His Needs,
Her Needs

Revised and Expanded Edition

His Needs,
Her Needs

BUILDING AN AFFAIR-PROOF MARRIAGE

Willard F. Harley, Jr.

Revell

a division of Baker Publishing Group
Grand Rapids, Michigan

© 1986, 1994, 2001, 2011 by Willard F. Harley, Jr.

Published by Revell
a division of Baker Publishing Group
P.O. Box 6287, Grand Rapids, MI 49516-6287
www.revellbooks.com

Printed in the United States of America

Library of Congress Cataloging-in-Publication Data
Harley, Willard F.
    His needs, her needs : building an affair-proof marriage / Willard F. Harley, Jr. — Rev. and expanded.
        p.   cm.
    ISBN 978-0-8007-1938-8 (cloth)
    ISBN 978-0-8007-2029-2 (intl. pbk.)
    1. Marriage—United States. 2. Communication in marriage—United States. 3. Married people—United States—Psychology. I. Title.
HQ734.H285 2011
646.7'8—dc22   2010040938

Scripture quotations are from the Holy Bible, New International Version®. NIV®. Copyright © 1973, 1978, 1984 by Biblica, Inc.™ Used by permission of Zondervan. All rights reserved worldwide. www.zondervan.com

14   15   16   17   7

To Joyce—
my one and only

Contents

Contents

Preface

In 1978 I was asked to teach a thirteen-week course on marriage at the church I attended. The topic was: what must a couple do to stay happily married? The Christian Education Director tape-recorded the course for me.

Over the next few years, I used those tapes in my counseling practice to support the advice that I gave couples. One couple volunteered to transcribe the tapes so that I could give them to other couples in written form.

In 1984 that rough transcription made its way into the hands of an employee of the Fleming H. Revell Publishing Company, that person passed it on to the acquisitions editor, and the rest is history. It was published in 1986 with the title *His Needs, Her Needs: Building an Affair-Proof Marriage.*

Within two years of its first printing, it became a bestseller and continues to be one of the most popular books on marriage right up to this year. It's been translated into twenty-two languages and more than three million copies have sold worldwide.

Finding a publisher for this book was the easy part—it almost fell into my lap. The hard part had been finding the answer to the question, what must a couple do to stay happily married?

Learning What Makes Marriages Succeed

When I was nineteen, a married acquaintance in college told me his marriage was in trouble and asked for my advice. The advice I gave did not help—his marriage ended in divorce. But my friend's marital failure started me thinking. What was wrong with the advice I gave? What makes some marriages succeed, and others, like my friend's, fail?

It was 1960, and I was about to witness something that few expected—the beginning of the end of the traditional nuclear family in America. Evidence of this social disaster accumulated over the next twenty years. The divorce rate climbed from about 10 percent to over 50 percent, and the percentage of single adults would go from 6.5 percent to 20 percent. While the divorce rate finally stabilized at about 45 percent in 1980, the percentage of single adults has continued to increase right up to the present. It is currently at about 50 percent and climbing because fewer and fewer people are willing to commit themselves to one partner for life.

At the time, I didn't know that my friend's marital failure was part of a trend that was about to overwhelm nuclear families. I was unaware of new cultural forces that would threaten marriages as never before. Marriage counselors had it easy prior to that time because people simply didn't divorce, regardless of how unhappy they were. But now, they were unwilling to tolerate a failed marriage. So if a marriage was to be saved, a counselor had to know what made marriages succeed. At the age of nineteen, I certainly did not have that answer.

Over the next few years, couples continued asking for my advice regarding marriage—especially after I earned a PhD degree in psychology. But I wasn't any more successful with them than I had been with my friend years earlier.

So I decided to become a marriage "expert." I enrolled in a two-year internship at a clinic that had one of the best reputations for marital therapy. I read books written by the most prominent marital theorists and practitioners, was supervised by the chairman of the University of Minnesota's Department of Family Social Science, and learned the latest techniques in helping spouses communicate with respect and understanding. But even after helping couples learn to communicate effectively, I was still unable to save their marriages. Almost everyone who came to me for help ended up like my college friend—divorced.

In my effort to become a marriage expert, though, I made a crucial discovery. I wasn't the only one failing to help couples. Almost everyone else working with me in the clinic was failing as well! My supervisor was failing, the director of the clinic was failing, and so were the other marriage counselors who worked with me.

And then I made the most astonishing discovery of all. *Most of the marital experts in America were also failing.* It was very difficult to find anyone willing to admit his or her failure, but when I had access to actual cases, I couldn't find any therapist who could prove that the counseling provided was any better than no counseling at all.

Many of these "experts" didn't even know how to make their own marriages work. Many had been divorced themselves—several times.

Marital therapy had the lowest success rate of *any* form of therapy at that time. In one 1965 study I read, less than 25 percent of those surveyed felt that marriage counseling did them any good whatsoever, and a higher percentage felt that it did them more harm than good. It seemed that marriage counseling made couples *more* likely to divorce.

What a challenge! Marriages were breaking up at an unprecedented rate, and no one knew how to help. So I stopped looking for answers from books, clinics, and experts, and started looking for them from those who came to me for answers—couples about to divorce.

I listened to spouses explain to me why they were ready to throw in the towel. I asked them, "What do you think it would take for you to be happily married again?"

The answer that came back to me was almost too simple to believe. Couple after couple explained to me that they married each other because they found each other irresistible—they were in love. But by the time they came to my office, they had lost that feeling for each other. In fact many were finding each other downright repulsive. When I asked them, "What would it take for you to be happily married again?" most couldn't imagine that ever happening. But when I persisted and couples were able to reflect on my question, the answer I heard repeated over and over was, "for us to be in love again."

If I wanted to save marriages, I would have to learn how to restore the feeling of love.

Discovering How to Restore Romantic Love

My background as a psychologist taught me that learned associations trigger most of our emotional reactions. Whenever something is presented repeatedly with a physically induced emotion, it tends to trigger that emotion all by itself. For example, if someone flashes the color blue and gives you an electric shock and then flashes the color red and gives you a soothing back rub, eventually the color blue will tend to upset you and the color red will tend to relax you.

Applying the same principle to the feeling of love, I theorized that it might be nothing more than a learned association. If someone of the opposite sex were to be present often enough when I was feeling particularly good, the person's presence in general might be enough to trigger an incredibly good feeling—romantic love.

I could not have been more correct in my analysis. I counseled the very next couple to do whatever it took to make each other feel good and avoid doing what made each other feel bad. They were able to restore their romantic love and their marriage was saved.

From that point on, I simply asked each spouse what the other could do that would make him or her the happiest. Whatever it was, that was their first assignment. Of course, not every couple really knew what would make them happy, and not every spouse was willing to do it. So I certainly wasn't successful with every couple.

But as I perfected my understanding of what it was that husbands and wives needed from each other to trigger the feeling of love, and learned how to motivate them to meet whatever need was identified, my rate of success skyrocketed.

Before long, I was helping almost every couple fall in love and thereby avoid divorce. My method proved to be so successful that I left my teaching position and started counseling full-time. As you can imagine, there were more couples wanting help from me than I could possibly counsel. It was then that I was asked to teach the thirteen-week course in my church: What must a couple do to stay happily married?

Twenty-five Years and Counting

Many have called this book the best book on marriage ever written. If that's true, it's not because I'm such a great writer. The poorest grades I earned in high school and college were in English and creative writing. This book has been successful because it shows couples how to restore and sustain their love for each other. And that's what a couple must do to stay happily married.

This book gets right to the heart of what makes marriages work—the feeling of love. In all my years as a marriage counselor, I've never counseled a couple in love who wanted a divorce. But I've counseled many divorcing couples with excellent communication and problem-solving skills who claim to care for each other.

Don't get me wrong—I'm very much in favor of improving communication and problem solving in marriage. And I'm certainly in favor of caring love. But unless communication and problem solving help trigger the feeling of romantic love, spouses feel cheated in their marriages and often want out.

Romantic love is a litmus test that reveals the right way for couples to demonstrate their caring love for each other. If you're in love, you are caring for each other the right way. If you're not in love, you should learn the right way to show your care. This book will teach you where to put your greatest effort to create and sustain romantic love.

Introduction

The purpose of this book is to teach you how to discover, and then learn to meet, each other's most important emotional needs. When you were first married, you assumed that those needs would be met, but for a variety of reasons, you've probably become very disappointed—perhaps disappointed enough to be tempted to let someone else meet your needs.

Usually ignorance contributes to this failure because men and women have great difficulty understanding and appreciating the value of each other's needs. Men tend to try to meet needs that they would value and women do the same. But the needs of men and women are often very different and by wasting effort trying to meet the wrong needs, a couple fails to make each other happy.

Husbands' and wives' needs are so strong that when they're not met in marriage, people are tempted to go outside marriage to satisfy them. And most of the people I've counseled have yielded to the temptation to violate their sacred vow to "forsake all others."

But aside from the risk of an affair, the most important emotional needs of a husband and wife *should be met* by each other for two other reasons. First, marriage is a very special relationship. Promises are made to allow a spouse the *exclusive* right to meet some of these important needs. When they are unmet, that is unfair to the spouse who must go through life without ethical alternatives.

But there is a second reason that I will explain more clearly in the pages of this book: when you meet each other's most important emotional needs, you create and sustain a feeling of love for each other that is essential in a successful marriage. I call that feeling *romantic love* and I want you both to experience it throughout your life together.

There's more to being in love than making each other happy, however. You must also know how to avoid making each other unhappy. That's why I've written a counterpart to this book, *Love Busters: Protecting Your Marriage from Habits That Destroy Romantic Love*. If you know how to make each other happy, but fail to avoid making each other unhappy, your skill and effort will be wasted. Spouses can learn to become each other's source of greatest pleasure when they meet each other's most important emotional needs. But they can also become each other's source of unbearable pain when they don't protect each other from instincts and habits that are common to all of us.

I've also written a workbook that will help guide you through the chapters of *His Needs, Her Needs* and *Love Busters*. It will help you identify the skills you should learn, and then encourage you to practice them until they become habits. This companion book is *Five Steps to Romantic Love: A Workbook for a Healthy Marriage for Readers of Love Busters and His Needs, Her Needs*.

I encourage you and your spouse to read these books together, complete the questionnaires, and answer the questions at the end of each chapter. You might even use two different-colored highlighters as you read, so each of you can let the other know what is most important to you. Keep these books in a place where you can refer to them regularly, because you should be reminded of the lessons they will teach you.

How Affair-Proof
Is Your Marriage?

1

When a man and woman marry, they share high expectations. They commit themselves to meeting certain intense and intimate needs in each other on an *exclusive* basis. Each agrees to "forsake all others," giving each other the exclusive right to meet these intimate needs. That does not imply that all needs are to be met by a spouse, but that there are a few basic needs that most of us strictly reserve for the marriage bond. Most people expect their spouse to meet these special needs, since they have agreed not to allow anyone else to meet them.

For example, when a man agrees to an exclusive relationship with his wife, he depends on her to meet his sexual need. If she fulfills this need, he finds in her a continuing source of intense pleasure, and his love grows stronger. However, if his need goes unmet, quite the opposite happens. He begins to associate her with frustration. If the frustration continues, he may decide she "just doesn't like sex" and he may try to make the best of it. But his strong need for sex remains unfulfilled. His commitment to an exclusive sexual relationship with his wife has left him with the choice of sexual frustration or infidelity. Some men never give in; they manage to make the best of it over the years. But many *do* succumb to

17

the temptation of an affair. I have talked to hundreds of them in my counseling offices.

Another example is a wife who gives her husband the exclusive right to meet her need for intimate conversation. Whenever they talk together with a depth of honesty and openness not found in conversation with others, she finds him to be the source of her greatest pleasure. But when he refuses to give her the undivided attention she craves, he becomes associated with her greatest frustration. Some women simply go through their married lives frustrated, but others cannot resist the temptation to let someone else meet this important emotional need. And when they do, an affair is the likely outcome.

His Needs Are Not Hers

When a husband and wife come to me for counsel, my first goal is to help them identify their most important emotional needs—what each of them can do for each other to make them happiest and most content. Over the years, I have repeatedly asked the question, "What could your spouse do for you that would make you the happiest?" I've been able to classify most of their responses into ten emotional needs—admiration, affection, conversation, domestic support, family commitment, financial support, honesty and openness, physical attractiveness, recreational companionship, and sexual fulfillment.

Obviously the way to keep a husband and wife happily married is for each of them to meet the needs that are most important to the other. But when I conducted all these interviews, I discovered the reason this is such a difficult assignment. Nearly every time I asked couples to list their needs according to their priority, men listed them one way and women the opposite way. Of the ten basic emotional needs, the five listed as most important by men were usually the five least important for women, and vice versa.

What an insight! No wonder husbands and wives have so much difficulty meeting each other's needs. They are willing to do for each other what they appreciate the most, but it turns out that their efforts are misdirected because what they appreciate most, their spouses appreciate least!

Pay careful attention to the next point I'm about to make, because it's one of the most misunderstood aspects of my program. Every person is unique. While men *on the average* pick a particular five emotional needs as their most important and women *on the average* pick another five, *any individual* can and does pick any combination of the basic ten. So although I have identified the most important emotional needs of the average man and woman, I don't know the emotional needs of any particular husband and wife. And since I'm in the business of saving individual marriages, not average marriages, you should identify the combinations of needs that are unique to your marriage. That's the reason I have provided a brief summary of the ten basic needs in appendix A of this book and the Emotional Needs Questionnaire in appendix B. These tools will help you identify the most important emotional needs unique to you and your spouse.

Often the failure of husbands and wives to meet each other's emotional needs is simply due to ignorance of each other's needs and not selfish un-willingness to be considerate. By learning to understand yourself and your spouse as totally unique people with particular emotional needs, you can identify your needs and communicate them to each other.

After each other's five most important emotional needs have been identi-fied, the next step is to become an expert in meeting your spouse's needs. That doesn't mean painfully gritting your teeth and making the best of something you hate. One spouse should never suffer to meet the emo-tional needs of the other. Instead, it means learning how to enjoy meeting emotional needs that are low on your list of priorities. In each chapter of this book, I'll offer suggestions as to how that objective can be achieved.

When spouses fail to meet each other's most important emotional needs, I have seen, strikingly and alarmingly, how they tend to choose the same pattern to satisfy their unmet needs: the extramarital affair. People wander into affairs with astonishing regularity, in spite of whatever strong moral or religious convictions they may hold. Why? When a spouse lacks fulfill-ment of any of the basic needs, it creates a thirst that must be quenched. If changes do not take place within the marriage to care for that need, the individual will face the powerful temptation to fill it outside of marriage.

If we are to make our marriages affair-proof, we cannot hide our heads in the sand. The spouse who believes his or her partner is "different" and, despite unmet needs, would never take part in an affair may receive a devastating shock someday. Instead, we need to understand the warning signs that an affair could happen, how such liaisons may begin, and how to strengthen the weak areas of a marriage in the face of such a relationship.

What Is an Affair?

Usually an affair consists of two people who become involved in an extramarital relationship that combines sexual lovemaking with feelings of deep love. However, it is possible to have an affair that involves only lovemaking or only the feeling of love toward someone outside of marriage. Although these types of affairs may also cause deep problems in marriage, my experience shows that they are more easily dealt with than the relationship that combines sex (usually very passionate sex) with the feeling of love. That relationship threatens the marriage to its core, because the lovers experience deep intimacy, and the affair meets at least one of the five most important emotional needs of the spouse outside the exclusive marital relationship. When one spouse discovers the other has broken the commitment of faithfulness, the marriage is shattered.

How Affairs Usually Start

An affair usually begins as a friendship. Your spouse may know the person who eventually becomes your lover as the husband or wife in a couple you consider "best friends." Or your lover may be someone you have met at work, church, or a community function.

Conversation draws you together. At first you talk about various topics of interest, but over time you begin to share personal problems with each other. As you spend more time together, you discuss more intimate problems, and eventually the problems you discuss reflect unmet emotional needs. As your friendship deepens, you start giving each other mutual support and encouragement, especially in regard to your unmet needs. Life is difficult. Many people become extremely disillusioned about the way their lives are turning out. When they find someone encouraging and supportive, the attraction toward that person acts as a powerful magnet.

Sooner or later, you find yourself in bed with your encouraging and supportive friend. It just seems to "happen." You don't intend to do it, and neither does your friend.

Very often the friendship that grows into an affair is very illogical. A wife will get a look at her husband's lover and exclaim, "How in the world could he be interested in *her*?" When a husband discovers his wife's lover, he wonders, "What could she be thinking?"

But the attraction is not logical; it's emotional. Based on the facts, the relationship stands no chance of succeeding, and very rarely does. What matters at the moment, however, is that the lover has been able to meet an unfulfilled need. He or she is regarded as the most caring person the wayward spouse has ever met, and a reciprocal desire to care for the lover is felt very deeply.

When you become involved in an affair, you and your lover seem to have an unconditional willingness to meet each other's emotional needs. This mutual desire to bring each other happiness at all costs builds an affair into one of the most satisfying and intimate relationships either of you have ever known. You respond sexually with ease and passion. You feel sure that no one else could ever be as exciting a partner as your new secret lover.

As the intensity of your mutual care and passion increases, you discover that you are caught in a trap of your own making. You lose all sense of judgment as you literally become addicted to each other in a relationship built on fantasy, not reality.

But as I mentioned earlier, the relationship is not logical; it's emotional. It's a fantasy. As you and your lover plan where and when to meet for passionate sessions of lovemaking, you leave the realities of everyday living behind.

It Could *Happen to You*

As I've discussed affairs and how they start, I may have offended you, at least a little bit, by using the second-person pronoun. But I used *you* for a specific reason. While most people would deny they could ever get involved in an affair, the hard truth is that, under certain conditions, any of us can fall victim.

It isn't particularly immoral people who fall into an affair. On the contrary, very normal men and women may get involved through a deceptively simple process. First, you let someone outside of marriage meet one of your most important emotional needs, say, intimate conversation. You may feel that there's no problem just talking to someone, especially if your own spouse doesn't seem interested in the problems you face.

Next, you find this friend to be particularly concerned for your welfare, and you begin to feel the same way toward your friend. The conversation turns to affection—the expression of care for each other.

From there, you begin to explain to each other what you need most in life, and you both express a desire to meet those needs for each other. The lovemaking that results seems so effortless and so natural that you believe you were made for each other. You think you've found your soul mate.

In some cases the process may take only a few weeks; in other cases it will take many years. But it happens with astonishing regularity. I have seen it happening in the lives of thousands of couples throughout my career. Sadly enough, it seems to make little difference what a person professes by way of religious commitment or moral values.

Often, in my early years as a counselor, I felt dismayed to see people with strong religious and moral commitments becoming involved in extramarital affairs. I am a church member myself, with strong convictions about the Christian faith. How could people who claim to have the same commitments go astray? Did their faith lack power?

But the more I dealt with unfaithful Christian clients and other people with deep moral convictions, the more I understood the power of our basic emotional needs. I came to see my own weaknesses and the strength of my own needs. When I married my wife, Joyce, I determined to be totally committed to her and to my marriage. I have remained true to my vows for the forty-eight years of our marriage, but not because I am some kind of iron-willed paragon of virtue. It's because Joyce and I have been realistic about meeting each other's important emotional needs. And we have never let someone outside of our marriage meet those needs.

In short, your needs keep score. To help you understand how this works, I'd like to introduce you to the Love Bank—an inner scoring device you probably never realized you had.

Why Your Love
Bank Never Closes

2

Unfortunately, most of us don't realize what we're getting into when we say, "I do." We think the dynamics of a good marriage depend on some mysterious blend of the "right" people. Or if a marriage turns out badly, we call the two people "wrong" for each other. While it's true that two inherently incompatible people *might* marry, it's unusual. More frequently, marital breakups occur when one or both partners lack the skills or awareness to meet each other's emotional needs. More often than not, being right or wrong for someone depends not on some mysterious compatibility quotient, but on how willing and able you are to meet that someone's needs.

What, then, if you are willing but unable or unskilled? Good news! You can do something about it. Retraining is possible at any time. For this reason I believe marriages that have been torpedoed by affairs need not sink. They can be towed into dry dock, repaired, and refitted. Once refitted, they will sail farther and faster than at any previous time.

But my ultimate goal is not salvaging marriages that have gone on the rocks of an affair. I reach well beyond that. I want to show you how to affair-proof your marriage by building a relationship that sustains romance and increases intimacy and closeness year after year. To make your marriage affair-proof, you need to know each other's basic needs and how to meet them. But first, I want to help you understand how needs become so powerful and all-consuming. As I said in the first chapter, needs keep score with relentless precision. To help my clients understand how this scorekeeping works, I have invented a concept that I call the Love Bank.

Everyone Has a Love Bank

Figuratively speaking, I believe each of us has a Love Bank. It contains many different accounts, one for each person we know. Each person makes either deposits or withdrawals whenever we interact with him or her. Pleasurable interactions cause deposits, and painful interactions cause withdrawals.

In my Love Bank system every deposit or withdrawal is worth a certain number of love units. If I meet a friend (we'll call him Jim), and the encounter leaves me feeling comfortable, 1 or 2 love units will be deposited in his account in my Love Bank. If the interchange makes me feel good, Jim's deposit in my bank may be 5 love units. Very good gets up to 10. But if he makes me feel exceptionally good the sky's the limit—20 or more can be deposited during one encounter.

Suppose, however, that I find myself feeling uncomfortable when I am with someone; we'll call her Jane. One or 2 love units are withdrawn from Jane's account. If she makes me feel bad, 5 units may be withdrawn. Very bad warrants a 10-unit withdrawal. If I consider my encounter with Jane among the worst experiences of my life, it may cost her a 20-unit withdrawal or more.

As life goes on, the accounts in my Love Bank fluctuate. Some of my acquaintances build sizable deposits. Others remain in the black but have small balances, perhaps because of fewer interactions with me. A third group builds up still smaller balances because my experiences with them are mixed—sometimes pleasant, sometimes painful. For these people, deposits almost equal withdrawals.

Other people go into the red with me. That means they cause me more pain than pleasure. I never feel good when I think of them and I do not want to see them or be with them. In short, their accounts in my Love Bank are overdrawn.

A Love Bank Love Story

Obviously, the Love Bank is not intended to be a mathematically accurate concept. It is simply designed to underscore the fact that we affect each other emotionally with almost every encounter. The accumulation of positive and negative experiences determines our emotional reaction to those we know. You are not actively aware of any of this, of course. You don't say to yourself, *Wow, that was a 15-unit deposit!* or, *Ugh! Minus 20 units for him*. Nonetheless, the love units keep coming in or going out.

Two Love Banks constantly operate in marriage: his and hers. Let's take a look at the story of John and Mary to see what can happen when a wife's account in her husband's Love Bank takes a huge dip and there is an understanding woman waiting in the wings down at hubby's office. In this example, we will concentrate on John's Love Bank, because he winds up having the affair.

When John meets Mary, he immediately feels something special. Not only is she beautiful, but she is charming, intelligent, and full of life. John's Love Bank instantly credits her account with 15 units.

A day or two later John calls Mary and asks her for a date. She accepts, and as John hangs up, 10 more units go into Mary's account.

On the date they have a fabulous time. John rates it as one of the best experiences of his life. Twenty more units added to Mary's account bring her balance to 45 love units. A second date is almost as good, and she gets 15 more love units, bringing the balance to 60.

But the next time John calls Mary for a date, she has to turn him down. She says she is truly sorry but she has a commitment she set up many weeks ago. She quickly adds that she is free the next night, if John would be interested. John is indeed interested and arranges to pick her up for dinner about eight o'clock.

What happens to Mary's account in John's Love Bank as a result of this slightly negative encounter?

She definitely sounded sorry she can't go out with me tonight, John muses. *I can't expect her to be available just any time. Besides, she did suggest that we go out tomorrow night. I'm sure she really likes me . . .* No matter how much John tries to reassure himself, the experience still leaves him feeling slightly uncomfortable. Mary's account in John's Love Bank is debited 1 unit.

Over the next few months John and Mary date regularly and often. The good and fabulous experiences far outnumber the occasional negative ones, and Mary's balance soon stands at 500 love units. Only Sarah, an old flame whom John broke off with more than a year ago, had ever accumulated more units in John's Love Bank. John begins to believe he is falling in love with Mary.

After six more months, Mary's balance stands at 1,000 love units, an all-time high total for any woman in John's life, well in excess of Sarah's score. At this point John feels he has never loved anyone as much as he loves Mary. He tells her she is the most attractive, intelligent, sensitive, charming, and delightful woman he has ever met.

Mary appeals to John so because of her balance in his Love Bank. He associates her with many positive—even fabulous—emotional experiences and only a few negative ones. John looks forward to each date with Mary, and his mind dwells on her when they are apart. He begins to wonder what he would do if he ever lost Mary. He can't imagine going through the rest of his life without her.

With Mary at my side, I wouldn't need anything or anyone else to be happy, John tells himself. Vivid thoughts of marriage form in his mind.

Meanwhile, John's account in Mary's Love Bank has grown steadily, but not at quite the same pace. When they met, Mary found John quite attractive. The first dates were very good experiences, and at this point she feels quite fond of him, but she still isn't sure. Mary remembers Bob and how much she liked him before he had broken off with her to marry an old friend from high school.

On their next date Mary abruptly tells John she needs a little breathing room. She suggests that they suspend their dating for a month or so and wonders if they shouldn't date other people during that time.

John feels devastated. This encounter registers as one of the all-time painful experiences of his life. Thirty units quickly come out of Mary's hefty account. A few days later John calls Mary and tries to convince her to change her mind, but she remains resolute. John tries calling back several times over the next week. Mary stands fast, and before John decides to leave her alone for a month, debits in Mary's account total 200.

John spends the month feeling miserable. He remains deeply in love with Mary, whose balance in his Love Bank still stands high at 800 units. John tries to date several other women, but they do not stand a chance. Because he is so crazy about Mary, he finds dating anyone else a negative experience. Through no fault of their own, all of John's dates accumulate nothing but debits in their accounts.

At the end of a month, John calls Mary. Her balance has remained at 800, because, while he has pined for her, there have been no further negative experiences to cause any more withdrawals. John feels ecstatic when Mary tells him that she has missed him terribly and accepts his invitation to go out the very next evening. All she needed, she says, was time to think things through and see clearly how she feels.

The first date after the monthlong separation is a memorable experience. Subsequent dates seem better than ever. At the end of the year, Mary's balance in John's Love Bank has risen to 2,000 units. At the same time, John's account in Mary's Love Bank has risen steadily and is at an all-time high of 1,100 units. John has eclipsed Bob in every way, and Mary also thinks of wedding bells.

One night, after dinner at their favorite restaurant, John proposes marriage. He tells Mary he wants to live his life for her happiness and assures her that if she will marry him, he will never do anything to hurt her. She accepts his proposal, and after a brief engagement, they become man and wife.

Beyond the Honeymoon

The first year of John and Mary's marriage is an extremely happy one. Without really thinking about it, they meet each other's basic needs quite well. John remains affectionate, patient, and as caring as he was when they dated. Mary responds passionately during lovemaking. They spend considerable time together and share their hopes and dreams in long conversations. Mary takes tennis lessons so she can keep up with John in his favorite recreational pastime.

Mary knows she can trust John because he is so honest in everything. John is proud of his attractive wife and feels particularly pleased with how she handles details around the house while still keeping her secretarial job on a part-time basis. John earns an excellent income as a computer analyst, but he and Mary have agreed she should work as much as she likes, at least for the present.

Mary feels secure with John, who gives every indication he loves being settled down with a home and family. She is proud of her husband and often tells him so.

During their first year of married bliss, what happens to the balances in each partner's Love Bank? Interestingly enough, John and Mary do not accumulate points at the rate they did before the marriage, mainly because they share a much wider variety of experiences than they had while dating. Now they are together when they feel good *and* when they feel bad. Credits and debits in their Love Bank accounts are being posted in accordance with the ups and downs of life.

In spite of the reduced rate of accumulation, Mary's balance in John's Love Bank still increases. At the end of their first year of marriage, her net gain from the previous year adds up to 100 units. That brings her overall total to 2,100. Approximately the same pattern holds true for John—his account increases to 1,200. During the next four years, accounts in both Love Banks continue to rise.

On their fifth anniversary, John still feels madly in love with Mary, and she feels the same about him. They decide to start a family, and little Tiffany arrives as they start their sixth year of marriage.

Critical changes start taking place in that sixth year. Mary is still the joy of John's life, but he notices an increase in his "down times." While Tiffany is a little doll and John loves her dearly, she creates new demands and negative experiences. Taking his turn to change baby's diaper in the middle of the night is not John's idea of a pleasant time. Also Mary's decision not to nurse Tiffany leaves John with his share of responsibilities to walk with her and hold the bottle. In addition, Mary has a tough time losing the weight she gained while she was pregnant.

As a net result of all these common little annoyances, Mary's balance in John's Love Bank drops by 100 units over the year. The loss is not that significant—yet. Mary's balance still remains very high, and John feels deeply in love with her.

But around the time of Tiffany's second birthday, Mary gets restless. She wants to be more than just a part-time secretary. She wants to have a more important career and doesn't want to wait until all of her children are grown and gone. She asks John if he would object if she returned to college, finished her bachelor's degree, and possibly went on for a master's in business administration.

"It will take six years of classes," Mary explains, "but I'll quit my part-time job so I can concentrate on the baby during the day and take most of the classes in the evening."

John agrees enthusiastically with her idea. His income is solid and stable, and they don't really need Mary's paycheck. He offers to babysit for Mary while she is at school and when she needs time on occasion to finish homework assignments.

Enter Noreen

Mary enrolls in classes and soon earns excellent grades. But those grades require sacrifice—and John's not too happy about it all. What bothers him most is that Mary rarely seems in the mood to make love. John understands her dilemma. School consumes a lot of energy, and what is left must be devoted to housekeeping and caring for Tiffany. By bedtime Mary feels exhausted, and John realizes that to insist on making love under those conditions would be inconsiderate.

John makes the best of it with less frequent and more hurried lovemaking when he finds Mary in the mood, but he also misses the attention she used to give him and the tennis games they always played on Saturday mornings. Now Mary seldom spends time with him, much less plays tennis on Saturdays. Instead, on the weekends, she always does the housework and catches up on homework assigned for Monday classes.

John and Mary continue in this pattern for the next two years. Mary's account in John's Love Bank drops slowly but steadily. John begins wondering what happened to the lovely and interesting creature he married. She seems lost in her books but never wants to discuss any of her classes with him. "It's all stuff you had years ago," Mary tells him. "Besides, you're a math expert, and I'm not taking that much math."

Note that John's account in Mary's Love Bank holds steady, because John is helping to meet a very special need in her life right now—getting an education. Mary realizes they haven't spent much time together but she deeply appreciates all John's sacrifices and his apparent total commitment to his family. *Things will be better as soon as I get my degree*, she tells herself. So Mary plunges on into academia, not quite realizing how her husband feels.

Meanwhile at work John spends more and more time with Noreen, an attractive product manager. The company transfers her to his department, and they start working together on a regular basis. When Noreen's husband leaves her for another woman, John tries to give her as much comfort and support as he can. Over the months John's friendship with Noreen deepens daily, and she soon has a few hundred units deposited in John's Love Bank.

Noreen makes deposits when they talk together at coffee and at other opportune moments. John has no qualms about sharing the good and the bad experiences of his life with Noreen. Their conversations sometimes remind him of the "old days" with Mary. So when John starts feeling frustrated due to Mary's lack of time for sex (or anything else but studying, it seems), he shares his frustration with Noreen and finds her quite sympathetic. In fact Noreen lets John know that since her divorce she feels sexually frustrated too.

The weeks and months fly by, and Mary finishes her bachelor's degree and launches into her master's program. "Only two more years and it's over," she tells John. "You've been wonderful to back me up like this."

John smiles and says he has been glad to do it, but inside he feels something else.

"She's just so wrapped up in that degree she can't think of anything else," John tells Noreen at coffee the next day. "I want her to have it but I'm wondering if the price has been too much to pay."

A few weeks later, Mary is particularly overwhelmed with studying for mid-term exams. At the same time, John gets hit with a special project that forces him into a great deal of overtime, and Noreen is working with him. One night as John and Noreen work late, alone, it happens. One moment

John is telling Noreen about how lonely he feels. The next moment she is in his arms, and they are making love.

When it's over and they are getting ready to go home for the night, John is visibly agitated and guilt ridden. Noreen senses his feelings and tells him she doesn't want to wreck his marriage or come between him and Mary. "Look," she says, "I have to be honest. I've fallen in love with you and I want to make you happy. Why don't we just make love together when we can? That's all I want."

An Unexpected Dilemma

On his way home John decides he doesn't feel so guilty after all. In fact he starts feeling elated. Through no fault of her own, Mary is unable at present to meet his sexual needs. Now Noreen wants nothing more than to fill in as a temporary sexual partner. *Why not let her, since it is helping meet her needs too?* John rationalizes. *It will all be temporary of course—until Mary is finished with school and can have more energy for sex.* Whatever guilt John feels he quickly quashes with a thought of his unfulfilled needs. From that time on, John and Noreen make love at least once a week and sometimes more often. In less than a year, Noreen's account in John's Love Bank jumps to 1,000 units, and Mary's has dropped to 1,000. He's in love with both women.

With no sexual frustrations, John's relationship with Mary improves a great deal. They include little Tiffany in everything they do together and make a special effort to enjoy family outings. When Mary has a brief break from studies and wants to make love, John is an enthusiastic partner. Those moments, unfortunately, do not happen very often.

Meanwhile John and Noreen work out their weekly rendezvous like a science. He never gives the morality of the situation a second thought. The huge project John has taken on has continued to demand overtime, and Mary never suspects a thing.

Actually Mary would have never known Noreen existed if it hadn't been for Jane, her good friend. Through another woman, whose husband works in John's division, Jane hears about how cozy he and Noreen are at coffee breaks. She gets suspicious and does a bit of snooping. She discovers John and Noreen's affair and goes right to Mary with the news.

At first, Mary does not believe Jane, but when she checks for herself, she catches John red-handed—and red-faced.

John is shaken because he never believed he'd be discovered. He figured that if Mary never knew about Noreen, she could never be hurt. For the first time, John feels deeply guilty. He begs Mary to forgive him and tries to explain why he did it. "I could see how hard you were working with your studies and I didn't want to be selfish and demand that we make love. The thing with Noreen just happened—then I guess I let it continue because I needed it. I never meant to hurt you. Now I can see that I was selfish after all and really stupid. I promise you it won't happen again."

Mary is heartbroken and furious. Why couldn't John have said something? Why did he have to betray their marriage to meet his needs? For the first time Mary sees that her drive for her degree has become a booby trap. She weeps uncontrollably, and John feels equally devastated. He continues to beg Mary for forgiveness and swears he will never see Noreen again.

Because she truly loves John, Mary forgives him and tries to make some changes. She cuts back on classes to make time for tennis again. She tries to make love to John several times a week, with passion and enthusiasm. John intends to be faithful, but in the first weeks after the confrontation, he suffers the most severe depression of his life. You see, whether or not he likes it, his Love Bank has taken its deposits. He now loves Mary *and* Noreen. John misses Noreen but he can't leave Mary. In short, John loves and needs both women. They both have substantial balances in his Love Bank, and he cannot seem to do without either one of them.

Hard as he tries, John cannot stay away from Noreen. To relieve his depression he gets back together with her and finds that she has also been depressed in his absence. She welcomes him back in a wild evening of lovemaking, and they plan more elaborate ways to get together without being discovered. But before long, Mary becomes suspicious and soon she knows she is sharing her husband with another woman, a woman to whom he has become addicted.

What Next?

Often at this point, people like John and Mary end up in my office. He wants to end the affair because of the growing pressure at home. She wants him to get rid of the other woman because it drives her crazy. And the other woman may have grown tired of being noble and patient. She pressures the husband to divorce his wife and marry her.

The erring spouse—in this case the husband—can't bring himself to give up either woman. He is like a donkey between two bales of hay, but instead of starving to death because he cannot decide which bale to choose, he tries to nibble on both!

Sometimes I am able to help and sometimes I am not. It all depends on whether the errant spouse and the lover can be separated permanently and the couple can learn to meet each other's basic emotional needs.

Whatever Happened to Commitment?

Maybe you're still asking yourself, *Should I be concerned that my spouse will have an affair if I don't meet her needs? Should my spouse fear that I might have an affair if my needs are not being met?* In reference to the needs described in this book, the answer is yes.

I realize this is not good news. "Whatever happened to commitment?" you may ask. "And what about *trust*? How can a marriage function if partners can't trust each other?"

I am all for commitment and I agree that trust is a vital bonding link in any marriage. But my experience with thousands of people has taught me an undeniable truth: if any of a spouse's five basic emotional needs goes unmet, that spouse becomes vulnerable to the temptation of an affair. By examining each of these areas of need separately, spouses can learn how to take care of each other in ways that will make their marriage resistant to affairs. More important, their marriage can become far more exciting and fulfilling—with more trust—than ever before.

In the first chapter I named ten emotional needs of men and women. While all ten are shared by both sexes, five tend to be rated by women as most important, and the other five are rated by men as most important. This disparity between men and women in regard to the priority of these ten needs makes it difficult for the two sexes to empathize with each other. "Why," each asks the other, "are these five things so important to you? None of them strikes me as so vital that I couldn't get along without them, at least for a while. What's the matter with you?"

Because of this lack of understanding, the couple unknowingly works at cross-purposes, each trying to fulfill the needs he or she feels, not the needs the mate feels. So wives may easily shower their husbands with affection because they appreciate it and want it so much themselves. Conversely, husbands smother their wives with sexual advances, because sex is one of their most pressing needs. Each becomes confused when, at best, the mate responds with mild pleasure and, at worst, becomes annoyed, irritated, or frigid.

This sort of behavior—in which one spouse gives the other something he or she doesn't need that badly—becomes self-defeating and destructive. Because the priorities of men's needs are different from the priorities of women's needs, each partner must take the time to discover and recognize the other's most important needs—those with the highest priority. Amazingly, many people think they can do this simply through intuition, but I'm convinced it can happen only as a result of clear communication and effective training.

The husband and wife who commit themselves to meet each other's most important needs will lay a foundation for lifelong happiness in a marriage relationship that is deeper and more satisfying than they ever dreamed possible.

In the next four chapters we will look at the two most important needs for most women (affection and intimate conversation) and the two most important needs for most men (sexual fulfillment and recreational companionship). We will start with the need for affection because when it's met, it lays the groundwork in meeting the need for sex.

In numerous counseling situations I have found men incredibly inept in regard to showing their wives affection. With few exceptions these men complain bitterly about "not enough sex." Meanwhile, their wives, who don't really understand how to have a fulfilling sexual relationship or how to enjoy making love, complain, "All he wants is my body; he never just wants to be affectionate." The frustration that results on both sides can easily lead to an affair and possible divorce. It need not be! Let me show you why.

3

The First Thing
She Can't Do
Without—Affection

When Jolene fell in love with Richard, she knew she had found her prince. At six feet three inches, Richard's 195 pounds were as lean and muscular at age twenty-three as they had been when Jolene admired him on the basketball court in high school. Ruggedly handsome, Richard was the strong, silent type, which only made him more intriguing to Jolene. Dates with Richard felt exciting, and when he held her in his arms, the passion level went right off the scale.

We've got the right chemistry, Jolene assured herself.

However, after just a few months of marriage, the passion began to pall. Jolene started noticing something a bit odd. Whenever she cuddled up for a hug or a little kiss, Richard became sexually aroused almost immediately. Nearly without exception, physical contact led straight to the bedroom.

Jolene learned also that Richard's "strong, silent" courting style had covered his tendencies for extreme moodiness and keeping almost everything to himself. Before they married, Richard had told Jolene that his mother had died when he was just ten, and his father and two older brothers raised him. She hadn't thought too much of it. That's probably why he's so rugged and manly, she told herself.

Jolene didn't realize that Richard had grown up in a home where displays of affection were infrequent before his mother died, and afterward they became almost nonexistent. He didn't know how to give affection because he had received so little himself. For Richard, affection in marriage was synonymous with sex, something that left Jolene feeling disillusioned and used. As their marriage approached its first anniversary, Richard's account in Jolene's Love Bank barely held its own.

At work, Jolene was transferred to a new department and there she met Bob, a warm and affable fellow who loved everyone. Bob had a habit of draping his arm over the shoulder of anyone he was walking with—male and female alike. No one took offense. He was just a friendly man who liked everybody.

Jolene noticed that she started to look forward to Bob's occasional hugs. They always made her feel good—warm and comfortable and cared for. One day they met in the hall. "Hi, Jolene, how ya doin'?" Bob greeted her as he gave her a little hug.

"You know, Bob," she said, "I've wanted to tell you for a long time how much I appreciate your hugs. It's nice to meet a man who likes to do that."

"Well, then, come here!" he laughed and gave her another hug and a little kiss on the cheek.

Jolene tried to act calm, but that little peck started her heart pounding. It continued pounding in the following weeks as she started receiving little notes from Bob. They were always tasteful and sweet. One said, "Good morning! Hope you have a great day! You're a fine person and you deserve the best. Your friend, Bob."

Jolene began to reciprocate with notes of her own. Before long she began to look forward to the arrival of Bob's latest note as the high point of her day. Sometimes he would bring her a little bouquet of flowers. That made her feel like a true princess.

They lunched together several times, and Bob's account in Jolene's Love Bank climbed steadily. Jolene found herself craving every expression of the gentle affection she received from Bob—the hugs, the smiles, the notes. Finally, she wrote a note to him: "I can't help it. I think I'm falling in love with you."

Bob didn't respond in kind but he continued to show Jolene kindness and affection. The weeks went by, and one day they found themselves alone together in a secluded spot they had chosen for a hurried lunch-hour picnic. As they packed up to leave, Jolene's hand touched Bob's, and she gave it a squeeze. Bob responded with an especially affectionate hug, and what followed came so naturally and beautifully Jolene couldn't believe it. Making love with Bob was the most exciting experience of her life, because she knew he cared so much for her.

In the following weeks they slipped off together as often as possible for passionate lovemaking. Having sex with Bob was wonderful, because Jolene could release all her emotions and become thoroughly involved. Bob's genuine affection made her feel loved and cared for as a person.

What had happened? Did Jolene's wedding vows mean nothing to her? Was she just waiting for her chance to two-time her husband? Hardly. Jolene simply felt so starved for affection that she was literally hugged into having an affair!

Affection—the Cement of a Relationship

To most women, affection symbolizes security, protection, comfort, and approval, vitally important commodities in their eyes. When a husband shows his wife affection, he sends the following messages:

- I care about you.
- You are important to me, and I don't want anything to happen to you.
- I'm concerned about the problems you face and I'll try to help you overcome them.

A hug can say any and all of the above. Men need to understand how strongly women need these affirmations. For the typical wife, there can hardly be enough of them.

I've mentioned hugging several times because I believe it is a skill most men need to develop to show their wife affection. It is also a simple but effective way to build their account in their wife's Love Bank.

Most women love to hug. They hug each other; they hug children, animals, relatives—even stuffed animals. I'm not saying they will throw themselves into the arms of just anyone. They can get quite inhibited about hugging if they think it could be misinterpreted in a sexual way. But the rest of the time, across most countries and cultures, women hug and like to be hugged.

Obviously a man can display affection in other ways that can be equally important to a woman. A greeting card or a note expressing love and care can simply but effectively communicate the same emotions. Don't forget that all-time favorite—a bouquet of flowers. Women, almost universally, love to receive flowers. Occasionally I meet a man who likes to receive them, but most do not. For most women, however, flowers send a powerful message of love and concern.

An invitation to dinner also signals affection. It is a way of saying to one's wife, "You don't need to do what you ordinarily do for me. I'll treat you instead. You are special to me, and I want to show you how much I love and care for you."

Jokes abound on how, almost immediately after the wedding, a wife has to find her own way in and out of cars, houses, restaurants, and so on. But a sensitive husband will open the door for her at every opportunity—another way to tell her, "I love you and care about you."

Holding hands is another time-honored and effective sign of affection. Walks after dinner, back rubs, phone calls, and conversations with thoughtful and loving expressions all add units to the Love Bank. As more than one song has said, "There are a thousand ways to say I love you."

From a woman's point of view, affection is the essential cement of her relationship with a man. Without it, a woman usually feels alienated from her mate. With it, she becomes tightly bonded to him, while he adds units to his account in her Love Bank.

But She Knows I'm Not the Affectionate Type

Women find affection important in its own right. They love the feeling that accompanies both the bestowal and the reception of affection, but men should understand that it usually has nothing to do with sex. It's the same emotion they exchange with their children or pets.

All of this confuses the typical male. Often he views affection as part of sexual foreplay, and usually it arouses him in a flash. Mistakenly he assumes that it has the same purpose and rapid effect on a woman. So the only time these men are affectionate is when they want to make love.

But this kind of affection does not communicate, "I care about you." Instead, it communicates, "I want sex." Instead of giving, it's taking. That selfish message is not lost on most women who crave affection. They deeply resent their husband's using such an important symbol of care *only* for the purpose of meeting his need for sex.

It gets much worse. Many men don't ever want to be affectionate. They don't think it should be necessary, even when having sex.

Let's look in on a hypothetical couple we'll call Briana and Bruce. There has been tension between them lately because Briana hasn't responded with much enthusiasm to Bruce's requests for sex. As our scene opens, she senses Bruce has that look in his eye again, and she tries to head him off at the pass. "Bruce, let's just relax for a few minutes. Then maybe you can hold my hand, and we can hug. I'm not ready for sex just like that. I need a little affection first."

Bruce bristles with a bit of macho impatience and says, "You've known me for years. I'm not the affectionate type and I'm not going to start now!"

Does this sound incredible or farfetched? I hear versions of it regularly in my office. Bruce fails to see the irony in wanting sex but refusing to give his wife affection. A man who growls, "I'm not the affectionate type," while reaching for his wife's body to satisfy his desires for sex, is like a salesman who tries to close a deal by saying, "I'm not the friendly type—sign here. I've got another appointment waiting." Although they shouldn't have a hard time understanding this simple logic, many men lose track of Harley's First Law of Marriage:

When it comes to sex and affection, you can't have one without the other.

Any Man Can Learn to Be Affectionate

Affection is so important for women that they become confused when their husband doesn't respond in kind. For example, a wife may call her husband at work, just to see if he's okay. She would love to receive such a call from him, but he never calls from work to see how she's doing. Doesn't he care about her? Her husband may care deeply for her but he doesn't express that care because his need for affection has a much lower priority than hers does.

When I go on a trip, I often find little notes Joyce has packed among my clothes. She is telling me she loves me, of course, but the notes send another message as well. Joyce would like to get the same little notes from me, and I have tried to leave such notes behind—on her pillow, for example—when I go out of town.

My need for affection is not the same as hers, nor is it met in similar ways. I've had to discover these differences and act accordingly. For example, when we walk through a shopping center, it is important to her that we hold hands, something that would not occur to me naturally or automatically. She has encouraged me to take her hand, and I'm glad to do so, because I know she enjoys that and it says something she wants to know.

When I try to explain this kind of hand-holding to some husbands in my counseling office, they may question my manhood a bit. Isn't my wife "leading me by the nose" so to speak? I reply that in my opinion nothing could be further from the truth. If holding Joyce's hand in a shopping center makes her feel loved and cherished, I would be a fool to refuse to do it. I appreciate her coaching on how to show affection. I promised to care for her when I married her and I meant every word of it. If she explains how I can best give her the care she wants, I'm willing to learn, because I want her happiness.

Almost all men need some instruction in how to become more affectionate, and those who have developed such loving habits have usually learned how to do so from good coaches—perhaps through a former relationship. In most marriages, a man's wife can become his best teacher, if he approaches her for help in the right way.

First, he needs to explain to her that he cares for her very much but often fails to express that deep care appropriately. Then he should ask her to help him learn to express this affection, which he already feels, in ways she will appreciate.

Initially she will probably feel puzzled by such a request. "When you love someone, affection comes naturally!" she may reply. She may not realize that affection comes more naturally for her than it does for him.

"I don't think I let you know how much I really care for you," he may answer. "I just assume you know, because I go to work, take you out, and help you around the house. I should be doing more to tell you how much I care about you."

"Sounds great! When do we start?"

She can help by making a list of the signs of care that mean the most to her. Women may express a need for physical closeness, such as hugging, hand-holding, and sitting close together. Kissing is very important to most women, as are token gifts and cards that express their husband's emotional attachment and commitment. Women love to have their husband take them out to dinner, and many wives regard any effort their husband makes to join them in shopping for food and clothing as a sign of affection.

When Ted and Paula came to my office for help to improve affection, I gave Paula a form to complete called the Affection Inventory (you can find that form in *Five Steps to Romantic Love*) to help her identify acts of affection that were most important to her. This form consists of two parts: "Affectionate Habits to Create" and "Affectionate Habits to Avoid." She completed the "Affectionate Habits to Create" section as follows:

- Hug and kiss me every morning while we're still in bed.
- Talk with me and tell me that you care about me while we're having breakfast together.
- Hug and kiss me before you leave for work.
- Call me during the day to see how I'm doing and to tell me you care about me.
- After work, call me before you leave for home, so that I can know when to expect you.

- When you arrive home from work, give me a hug and kiss and spend a few minutes talking to me about how my day went (I'll talk to you about how your day went too).
- Help me with the dishes after dinner.
- Hug and kiss me for at least five minutes when we go to bed at night and tell me that you care about me.
- Bring me flowers once in a while as a surprise (be sure to include a card that expresses your care for me).
- Remember my birthday, our anniversary, Christmas, Mother's Day, and Valentine's Day. Give me a card and gift that is sentimental, not practical. Learn how to shop for me.

Under the heading "Affectionate Habits to Avoid," she wrote:

- Don't tell me how attracted you are to my body when you want to express your affection.
- Don't touch my butt, breasts, or crotch when you are being affectionate with me (especially when we are washing the dishes together).

Ted could understand what Paula meant in her list of "Affectionate Habits to Create." And he was willing to try to learn to be more affectionate by practicing those behaviors until they became habits. But he was confused, and somewhat offended, with her entries in "Affectionate Habits to Avoid."

"Don't you want me to tell you how sexy you look to me? You turn me on, and I'm just following my instincts," he admitted.

"I want to be attractive to you," she replied. "But when we're together, you seem to be interested only in my body. It makes me feel that you don't care about me as a person."

I explained to Ted the difference between affection and admiration (that we will cover in chapter 12). Affection is the communication of care, while admiration is the communication of appreciation, value, and respect. He was certainly able to communicate his appreciation for the way Paula looked, but this didn't communicate his care for her.

Paula was starved for affection, which was her most important emotional need. Admiration, on the other hand, was far down her list of needs that she wanted Ted to meet. Granted, some women with a high-priority need for admiration want their husband to tell them how attractive they are. And some don't even mind being fondled while washing dishes as evidence of that admiration. But Ted's failure to provide affection combined with Paula's very low need for admiration made her feel particularly uncared for when he focused most of his attention on her physical attributes.

After helping Ted understand what Paula considered to be affection, and what was not affection, I gave him a plan to turn those affectionate behaviors into habits. The strategy required him to keep with him at all times the list of affectionate behaviors Paula craved. Every day the list reminded him of what she wanted him to do for her. From the moment he woke up in the morning hugging and kissing her to the five-minute hug before they went to sleep at night, he was meeting her need for affection. Eventually, the list was unnecessary. Ted was in the habit of being an affectionate husband.

If your wife identifies affection as one of her most important emotional needs, and wants you to learn to meet that need for her, follow the plan that I used for Ted. Once your wife has helped you identify habits that will meet her need for affection and habits she would like you to avoid, create a plan that sees to it you'll become an affectionate husband.

To repeat a point I make throughout this book: knowing what your spouse needs does not meet the need. You must learn new habits that transform that knowledge into action. Then and only then is that need met. Don't build up your wife's hopes with your good intentions. Go one step further and learn the habits of affection. If you know your wife's needs and then fail to deliver, your relationship will be worse than it was before you gained understanding. At least then you could plead ignorance!

Habits usually take time to develop—sometimes weeks, sometimes months. Your plan should include the time you expect to be "in training." The easiest habits to learn are those that you enjoy performing, the most difficult are the ones you tend to find uncomfortable. At first, most changes of behavior seem and look awkward. They're not spontaneous and smooth; they're contrived. This is especially true for many habits of affection. For this reason many people give up too quickly trying to develop these habits. But you'll find that after a behavior has been repeated a number of times, it becomes more natural and spontaneous. What begins as uncomfortable can become second nature to you.

Another obstacle is that habits of affection are not necessarily motivated by your own need; they are motivated by your desire to meet your wife's need. She may be offended at first, when you're not as interested in affection as she is. But eventually, you will find that you enjoy your time of affection together, and when that happens, she won't be concerned about how it developed. You'll both be winners. She will have what she needs from the man who enjoys meeting the need.

Sex Begins with Affection

Over the years I have seen nothing more devastating to a marriage than an affair. Sadly enough, most affairs start because of a lack of affection (for the wife) and lack of sex (for the husband). It's quite a vicious cycle. She doesn't get enough affection, so she shuts him off sexually. He doesn't get enough sex, so the last thing he feels like being is affectionate.

The solution to this tragic cycle is for someone to break it. I made my reputation as a marriage counselor convincing wives that if they met their husband's sexual need, their husband would be willing to meet their need for affection in return, and any other needs, for that matter. It worked so well that I built a thriving practice almost overnight.

But it can also be done the other way around. A husband can meet his wife's need for affection first. I've discovered that when her need is met, she's usually much more willing to meet his need for sex. Since I begin this book with the wife's need for affection, I recommend to husbands that, if their need for sex is not being fulfilled, they should take the initiative by learning to meet their wife's need for affection first.

Affection is the *environment* of the marriage, while sex is an *event*. Affection is a way of life, a canopy that covers and protects a marriage. It's a direct and convincing expression of care that gives the event of sex a more appropriate context. Most women need affection before sex means much to them.

Because men tend to translate affection into sex so readily, I emphasize learning sexless affection. I try to teach a husband to make affection a nonsexual way of relating to his spouse. He learns not to turn it on just to get some sex. Whenever he and his spouse come together, a big hug and kiss should be routine. In fact almost every interaction between them should include affectionate words and gestures. I believe every marriage should have an atmosphere that says, "I really care about you and I know you care about me."

When I talk about sexless affection, many men become confused. What is he supposed to do with his natural feeling of sexual arousal, which can be triggered by almost any act of affection? He wants to know if he has to "take cold showers" to keep cool. I point out to him that when he was dating, he was just as sexually aroused as he is now, even more so! But he showed plenty of affection and attention that did not include groping and grabbing. He treated the young lady with respect and tenderness.

Many husbands remember the passionate encounters of their courting days and want to know, "Why doesn't she get turned on the way she did before we were married?"

Patiently I explain that they aren't treating their wife the way they did back then. After marriage they thought they could do away with the preliminaries and get right to the main event. But it turns out that the "preliminaries" are not only required for a fulfilling sexual relationship, they're also needed in their own right. It may be that what they think are preliminaries are her "main event."

In most cases, a woman needs to feel emotionally bonded with her husband before she has sex with him. Sex for her becomes a physical expression of that emotional bond. She achieves this feeling through the exchange of affection and undivided attention.

Her need for this one-spirit unity helps us understand how affairs develop. In the typical affair, a woman has sex with a man after he has demonstrated his care for her by showering her with affection. Because his expression of care makes her feel emotionally united with him, the physical union is usually characterized by a degree of ecstasy otherwise unknown to her in a marriage that lacks affection. She concludes that her lover is right for her because she doesn't feel the same way when she makes love to her husband.

In truth, any marriage can have the sizzle of an affair if it has that strong one-spirit bond. It's a tragic misperception for her to think that her husband is not right for her based on a comparison of feelings at a moment in time. If he were to lay the groundwork with affection, their bond would be restored and the affair would be seen for what it really is—a misguided effort to have an important emotional need met.

As I mentioned earlier, just as men want their wife's sexual response to be spontaneous, women prefer their husband's affection to be spontaneous. But when we try to develop new behavior, it seems contrived and unnatural. At first, efforts to be affectionate may not be very convincing and, as a result, may not have the effect that spontaneous affection does. But with practice, the affectionate behavior eventually conveys accurately the feeling of care that a husband has for his wife. That, in turn, creates the environment necessary for a more spontaneous sexual response from her.

A woman's need for affection is one of her deepest emotional needs. But all that I've said here will prove of little value if a wife fails to understand that her husband has an equally deep need for sex. In the next chapter I'll confront the woman in an effort to explain why, for men, sex is not just one of several ways to end a lovely evening. To the typical man, sex is like air or water. He can't do without it very well.

If a wife fails to understand the power of the male sex appetite, she will wind up having a husband who's tense and frustrated at best. At worst, someone else may step forward to meet his need and, tragically enough, that happens all too often in our society. But it can all be avoided if husbands learn to be more affectionate and wives respond with more eagerness to make love. As Harley's First Law of Marriage says:

When it comes to sex and affection, you can't have one without the other.

Questions for Him

1. On a scale of one to ten, with ten being "very affectionate," how affectionate are you toward your wife? How would she rate you?

2. In what specific ways do you show your wife affection?
3. Would you be willing to have her coach you in how to show her more affection in the ways she really likes?

Questions for Her

1. Is affection as important to you as this chapter claims?
2. If you're not getting enough affection from your husband, are you willing to patiently coach him?
3. Would you find it much easier to make love if you felt emotionally bonded to your husband and felt that he truly cared about you?

To Consider Together

1. Do you need to show more affection to each other? If so, are you willing to learn to be affectionate in ways that best communicate your care for each other?
2. Is there reluctance on either one's part to be affectionate? If so, why and what can you both do to overcome that reluctance?
3. Make a list of "affectionate habits to create" and a list of "affectionate habits to avoid." Practice them until they become spontaneous and almost effortless.

The First Thing
He Can't Do
Without—Sexual Fulfillment

4

"Before we married, Jim was so romantic and affectionate—a regular Don Juan. Now he seems more like Attila the Hun."

"When John wants sex, he wants it right now. He doesn't care how I feel; all he cares about is satisfying himself."

"Bob has turned into an animal. All he can ever think about is sex, sex, sex!"

When I hear wives make remarks like these in my counseling office, I understand how disillusioned they must feel. At one time men who knew how to be affectionate swept these women off their feet. But once committed in marriage, all that affection vaporized, and what was left seemed like pure lust. Was the affection during courtship simply a ploy to captivate a woman for sexual gratification?

"Why do you think your husband acts the way he does?" I ask.

"Because he doesn't really care about me. All he cares about is sex" is the usual answer—or words to that effect.

These women share a real and very widespread problem. I describe it simply in Harley's First Corollary:

The typical wife doesn't understand her husband's deep need for sex any more than the typical husband understands his wife's deep need for affection.

Marriage is a very conditional union. If a husband does not try to meet his spouse's needs, and she does not try to meet his, they may be technically married but they will not know the happiness and fulfillment marriage should provide. But if both sides want to listen to each other and change, a couple can solve their problems without much difficulty.

In chapter 3, I was fairly hard on the men, because I believe wholeheartedly that their inability to show affection is such a crucial problem. Remember, *affection is the environment of the marriage; sex is the special event*. At the same time, a wife must grasp just how special a man finds sex. He isn't "pawing and grabbing" at her because he has turned into a lusting monster. He is pawing and grabbing because he needs something—very badly. Many men tell me they wish their sex drive wasn't so strong. As one thirty-two-year-old executive put it, "I feel like a fool begging her all the time but I can't help it. I *need* sex."

Why Men Feel Cheated

When a man chooses a wife, he promises to remain faithful to her for life. This means that he believes his wife will be his only sexual partner "until death do us part." He makes this commitment because he trusts her to be as sexually interested in him as he is in her. He trusts her to be available to him whenever he has a need for sex, just as she trusts him to meet her emotional needs.

Unfortunately, in many marriages, the man finds that putting his trust in this woman has turned into one of the biggest mistakes of his life. He has agreed to limit his sexual experience to a wife who is unwilling to meet that vital need. He finds himself up the proverbial creek without a paddle. If his religious or moral convictions are strong, he may try to make the best of it. Some husbands tough it out, but many cannot. They find sex elsewhere.

The unfaithful man justifies his behavior in terms of his wife's failure to keep her sexual commitment to him. When she discovers his unfaithfulness, she may try to "correct her error" and improve their sexual relationship, but by then it may be too late. She feels hurt and resentful, and he has become deeply involved in an affair.

One of the strangest studies in human behavior is the married man who is sexually attracted to another woman. He seems possessed. I have known bank presidents, successful politicians, pastors of flourishing churches, leaders in every walk of life who have thrown away careers and let their life achievements go down the drain for a special sexual relationship. They explain to me in no uncertain terms that without this relationship everything else in life seems meaningless to them.

I sit and listen to these pathetic and bewildered men so motivated by their need for sex that their reasoning capacities have turned to mush. Ordinarily I would tend to admire these intelligent, successful, and otherwise responsible individuals. But their misdirected sex drive has them completely unraveled.

While this sequence of events is an insane way to live, my counseling experience leads me to believe that more than half of all married couples go through the agony of unfaithfulness and affairs. I believe that most couples can easily prevent this tragedy. Prevention begins with an understanding of the differences between the sexuality of men and women.

What's the Difference?

There are three important differences between men and women when it comes to sex. The first involves their sexual drive; the second, awareness of their sexuality; and the third, their primary reason to have sex.

Sexual Drive

Regarding the first difference, sexual drive, we all know that the average man has a much higher sex drive than the average woman. This is because the only known aphrodisiac, testosterone, flows in abundance through men while in much shorter supply in women. A woman can witness firsthand what an intense sex drive feels like by wearing a testosterone patch for a week to raise her level of the hormone to that of the average nineteen-year-old male. It's an eye-opening experience for women, who usually don't want to repeat it.

While a man's sex drive is not the only reason he has a need for sexual fulfillment, it's the most important reason that it's usually his number one emotional need. But over a lifetime, the level of testosterone in a man's bloodstream decreases about 1 percent a year, which makes him less sexually motivated and less able to perform as he ages. For this reason older men don't necessarily rank sexual fulfillment as important as they did earlier in life.

Sexual Awareness

The second difference, awareness of their sexuality, contributes mightily to the sexual problems faced early in marriage. I use the term *sexual awareness* to convey an understanding of one's own sexual experience—knowledge of how to respond sexually. Over the years, I have collected more than forty thousand questionnaires from clients, which ask about their sexual history and sexual behavior. From the results of these questionnaires, it is apparent that almost all men masturbate, and many start at a very young age (eight to ten). On the other hand, girls who masturbate begin much later, most often in late teens and early twenties, and more than half the women we've surveyed had never masturbated at all.

The first heterosexual experiences reported by the men and women we surveyed took place at essentially the same ages (between thirteen and sixteen). But their reports of that experience differed remarkably. Almost every man surveyed enjoyed his first heterosexual encounter, while most women reported finding it a disappointment. The men know how to respond sexually, while the women haven't figured it out yet.

I believe at least part of this discrepancy lies in the differences in their sex drive. For the most part, boys are greatly helped by a strong sex drive and a history of sexual responsiveness through masturbation, while girls do not come to that first encounter with much of a sexual history at all. Many do not know what to expect. A desire to be liked by their boyfriend or curiosity—"What *is* the big deal about sex, anyway?" they ask—motivates them, but not the feeling of an urgent need for sexual gratification.

This disparity in terms of sexual drive and experience lies at the root of many marital problems, even in this day of supposed sexual liberation and enlightenment. Young men and women come together in marriage from opposite ends of the spectrum. He is more sexually experienced and motivated by strong desires; she is less (often much less) experienced, less motivated, and sometimes naive. Furthermore, his experience is so visceral and almost automatic that he usually does not understand that most women must learn how to respond sexually, and he is not prepared to teach his bride how to enjoy her own sexuality. He just knows how much he loves it and assumes that what he enjoys must feel at least as good to her. Most young husbands discover the falsehood of that assumption before very long; they learn the frustrating truth that the wonderful sexual discoveries they have made seem much less meaningful to their bride. For many men this becomes a source of unparalleled frustration.

A man cannot achieve sexual fulfillment in his marriage unless his wife is sexually fulfilled as well. While I have maintained that men need sex more than women, unless a woman joins her husband in the sexual experience, his need for sex remains unmet. Therefore a woman does her husband no favors by sacrificing her body to his sexual advances. He can feel sexually satisfied only when she joins him in the experience of lovemaking.

But I've counseled many wives who are fully aware of their own sexuality and yet refuse to make love to their husband. They tell me that when they do make love to him, they have no problem becoming sexually aroused and reaching a climax, often responding faster than he does. Yet they won't do it. This common problem is due to the third difference between men and women—their primary reason to have sex.

Sexual Motivation

A very important question to ask your spouse is, "Why should we make love?" If the husband is honest, he will answer with something to the effect that making love relieves his sexual craving. But the answer of most wives is very different. She will say that sex helps her feel closer to her husband. For her, it is all about intimacy and emotional bonding.

So can you see why a woman who enjoys sex would refuse to make love to her husband? If she doesn't feel emotionally close to him, she won't want to make love to him. He has probably failed to communicate his care for her (lack of affection) or he's proven that he doesn't care by ignoring her completely—until he feels like having sex. Women who are emotionally withdrawn from their husband are notoriously unwilling to have sex with him. Men, on the other hand, rarely turn down an opportunity to have sex with their wife, even when they feel totally disconnected.

As soon as you understand these three differences in the sexuality of men and women, you will be able to logically address just about any sexual problem you face. Negotiation begins with a respectful exchange of perspectives, and by discussing these differences with each other and searching for ways to make sex fulfilling for both of you, you will be able to find a solution to one of the most common problems in marriage.

How to Achieve Sexual Compatibility

Let's review once more the three important differences between men and women when it comes to sex:

1. *Sexual drive.* The abundance of the aphrodisiac hormone, testosterone, in men and relative lack of it in women gives men a much greater craving for sex.
2. *Sexual awareness.* Boys tend to explore their sexuality earlier and more often than girls. By the time they marry, they usually have a better understanding of how to have a fulfilling sexual experience.
3. *Sexual motivation.* With a much higher sex drive, the primary reason men have sex is to relieve their craving. For women, the primary reason is intimacy and emotional bonding.

To help you develop sexual compatibility in your marriage, I will address all three of these important differences as I present a quick lesson in human sexuality. While some of this material may seem a bit unromantic

54

and clinical, bear with me. The better you understand the following information, the better you can meet each other's needs sexually.

Most sexual conflicts are resolved when a husband and wife learn what actually happens—emotionally and physiologically—when they make love to each other.

The sexual experience divides into five stages: *willingness, arousal, plateau, climax,* and *recovery.*

The first stage, *willingness,* gets the ball rolling. The husband's willingness is usually motivated by sexual desire, while the wife is motivated by her emotional connection to him. During *arousal,* he and she begin to sense sexual feelings. His penis usually becomes erect, and her vagina secretes lubricating fluid. If his penis and her clitoris are stimulated properly through intercourse or manual stimulation, they pass into the *plateau* stage. In this stage his penis becomes very hard and her vagina contracts involuntarily, providing greater resistance and a heightened sensation during intercourse. The *climax,* which lasts only a few seconds, is the peak of the sexual experience. At this time the penis ejects semen in bursts (ejaculation), and the vagina alternately contracts and releases several times. The *recovery* period follows, in which both partners feel peaceful and relaxed; the penis becomes soft, and the vagina, no longer secreting lubricating fluid, relaxes.

While men and women experience the same five stages, they do not do so in the same physical and emotional ways. Usually what works for a man does not work for a woman, and usually what works for a woman does not work for a man. Couples who wish to experience sexual compatibility need to appreciate and understand the differences. I will discuss each stage of the sexual response separately and highlight some of the most important differences.

Willingness—How It All Starts

I have already said that most men are motivated to have sex because of a sexual craving created by their relatively high levels of testosterone. Women, on the other hand, are generally motivated by emotional closeness. Granted, women also experience a craving for sex, but it usually occurs only once or twice a month, while many men experience it almost daily. So men are generally willing to have sex whenever their wife offers it because of ongoing sexual desire. But women are willing to have sex when their husband offers it only if they feel emotionally close to him.

The reason most women are willing to have sex with their husband is that they want to express their love for him in this way. But they don't like to call it sex. They consider it "making love." They want to extend their affection, which is the expression of their care, into lovemaking. That's the reason affection is the *environment* that makes the *event* of sex attractive to most women. They are willing to make love if their husband is affectionate.

There's another reason a woman is willing to make love. She anticipates a mutually enjoyable sexual experience with her husband. And that's possible only if he understands how she can enjoy the remaining four stages of the sexual experience and applies that understanding to their lovemaking.

In most cases, an environment of affection and anticipation of a mutually enjoyable sexual experience result in her willingness to make love to him whenever he has a sexual desire.

Arousal—the Beginning of Sexual Feelings

Most men can become sexually aroused in a variety of ways, but the hands-down favorite is visual. Numerous magazines, calendars, films, videos, and so on that feature nude or barely clad women all cash in on one thing: men like to look at naked women. During counseling sessions, wives readily testify that their husband enjoys watching them undress and that, when they are naked, his arousal follows in just a few seconds.

A man experiences arousal easily, and it may happen several times a day. Many nonvisual and visual experiences can do it: a scent of perfume in an elevator, watching a woman's walk, looking at a photo of a scantily clad woman, or even daydreaming.

Sometimes wives express dismay at their husband's ability to be sexually aroused by other women but they need to understand that their husband is not being promiscuous or unfaithful. He is simply experiencing a characteristic male reaction. Arousal in itself doesn't mean that much to a man. It may occur relatively effortlessly, and he sometimes experiences it whether or not he wants to.

Women may find this hard to understand, because they experience arousal so differently from the way men do. Much more complicated and deliberate, the woman's excitement does not, in most cases, depend on visual stimulation. Although male centerfolds in women's magazines get a lot of attention, most women really think of them more as humorous conversation pieces than a means of genuine sexual stimulation.

For most men, sexual desire leads to sexual arousal so effortlessly that they don't consider them to be two separate stages. For most women, however, the two are quite different. Arousal usually doesn't take place unless there is a deliberate decision to let it happen.

If a woman is willing to make love, she will encourage her husband to touch her in ways that lead to her arousal. But if she's not willing, the same touching usually leads to a very defensive and angry reaction. In other words, only her willingness gives him the right to do what it takes to arouse her sexually.

Once a woman is willing to be aroused, she's ready to receive and respond to appropriate tactile stimulation, such as the caressing of her body (especially the breasts and nipples) and stimulation of the area surrounding the clitoris. I usually encourage a couple to avoid intercourse until the woman is sexually aroused. By then, her vagina is well-lubricated, and the risk of an uncomfortable entry is greatly reduced. She is also more responsive to intercourse when she is aroused.

When intercourse begins, a woman needs to sustain strong stimulation to her clitoris and vaginal opening. A woman learns to create this more intensive stimulation by (1) contracting her pubococcygeus (PCG) muscle (it is the muscle used to stop urine flow), which tightens the vagina on the inserted penis; (2) thrusting her pelvis rapidly; (3) and assuming a position that increases pressure on the clitoris and resistance to the penis in the vaginal opening.

The shorter the distance between a woman's clitoris and the tip of her vaginal opening, the easier it is for her to be sexually stimulated by intercourse. A distance less than one-half inch generally makes stimulation almost effortless, while a distance of more than one inch can be challenging. But those with a clitoris-vagina distance greater than one inch can find intercourse to be a very satisfying sexual experience if they experiment with various positions until they find one that works for them. When they find that position, their husband should not try to deviate from it.

As I implied earlier, if a husband wants his wife to be a willing sex partner, he should guarantee that each sexual experience be enjoyable for her. So she should be able to tell him what he can do to achieve that objective, and he should do it for her. Since he enjoys a much broader range of sexual positions and techniques than she, he should limit them to what they both enjoy. Usually that means discovering what she enjoys most and sticking to it.

With lovemaking in mind, I highly recommend that spouses be affectionate while becoming sexually aroused. It's not just sex. It's a bonding experience, especially for most women. So spouses should kiss each other, hug each other, and look at each other. If the way you have sex prevents you from being affectionate, your wife is less likely to be willing the next time.

Plateau—the Best Stage of Lovemaking

A few minutes of intense physical stimulation usually brings an aroused woman (and her aroused husband) to the next stage—the sexual plateau. In arousal, a hard penis must be voluntarily made hard, and a loose vagina must be voluntarily tightened to have the best effect. But in the plateau stage, the penis is hard and the vagina is tight involuntarily. A man can't relax his penis and a woman can't loosen her vagina. The sexual pleasure experienced in this stage is intense and can be maintained indefinitely.

While women need very special and intense stimulation to reach a plateau, men need much less stimulation. Intercourse itself is almost always sufficient for men, and many reach a plateau with even less stimulation.

Unfortunately, her need for more stimulation and his need for less create a common sexual problem: premature ejaculation, which means that he comes to a climax too soon. As she thrusts quickly to stimulate herself to the plateau, the stimulation becomes too great for him. He experiences a climax and loses his erection before she can reach a plateau or climax.

On the other hand, if a man tries to hold back a climax, he may find himself falling from the plateau stage, back to arousal, and his penis softens. Although he may continue intercourse, his penis is not hard enough to give his wife the stimulation she needs.

For many men, maintaining the plateau stage without rising to a climax or receding to arousal is a challenge. When having intercourse, the husband must hold the plateau about ten minutes, the time his wife needs to reach the plateau. Then she may need another five minutes to experience a climax. Men commonly climax before their wives have enough stimulation to enjoy the plateau or reach climax. Even the best intentioned man needs training to achieve this goal.

Recent discoveries in medical science to help men maintain a hard erection have been very successful. While originally designed for aging men who have developed impotence (failure to maintain an erection), men as young as twenty-five are now finding that these medications help them create a consistently enjoyable sexual experience. I have recommended these medications to many of my clients who have had problems maintaining a hard erection during intercourse.

The Climax—Ecstasy or Anxiety?

Many consider the climax (or orgasm) as an ecstatic experience that both partners should try to reach simultaneously for optimal pleasure. Because of this popular idea, many people have a distorted view of the climax, and some couples, in an effort to reach their goal of climaxing together, lose out on the pleasure of the entire lovemaking experience. When a couple feels anxiety rather than an enjoyment of each other, they are putting too much importance on performance and not enough on the pleasure of their lovemaking.

The woman who knows how to reach a plateau is only one small step away from reaching a climax; it takes only a little more time and stimulation. However, some women I've counseled have confided in me that they really don't find reaching climax worth the effort it takes to do so. They have reached it at times, but they are quite happy with the sex act without an orgasm and wish their husband would not try to pressure them to climax. Generally I encourage men to let their wife decide whether or not to experience climax.

In my practice I have observed that women with an abundance of energy usually choose to climax whenever they make love. Women with less energy or women who feel tired after a long, hard day often choose not to climax.

Men, on the other hand, whether full of energy or exhausted, almost always choose to climax, because it requires such little additional effort.

A good sexual relationship takes this difference of effort into account. A sensitive man will not put pressure on his wife to climax, because he realizes she may enjoy sex more without it. Anxiety over whether or not to climax has no place in a fulfilling sexual relationship.

Recovery—Afterglow or Resentment?

An appropriate description of the recovery phase is an afterglow, with both partners lying in each other's arms, feeling completely fulfilled. But because men and women do not share the same instincts after a climax, this ideal state eludes many couples.

Characteristically, following a climax, a woman falls back into the plateau stage and can reach another climax, if she so chooses. If she does not decide to climax again, she slowly falls back to arousal and then finally to an unaroused level. As this takes place, she feels a deep sense of peace come over her and generally has a deep desire for continuing affection. Many women I counsel report that this feeling may remain for up to an hour after intercourse.

During the recovery period, most men do not experience the same feelings. A second climax for men is not as desirable because it requires much more effort than the first, if a man can achieve it at all. For most men a third climax within a short period of time is nearly impossible. Unlike the woman, the man does not fall back to the plateau after climax—usually he falls back into arousal, and even that is short lived. Within minutes of a climax, many men are totally uninterested in sex. Often such men will jump up and take a shower or roll over and go to sleep. Many a honeymoon has been destroyed by such insensitive behavior.

Each couple must work out for themselves a proper sense of timing at the recovery stage. A man should be ready to bring his wife to another sexual climax through digital stimulation if she chooses, or he should continue showing her affection for at least fifteen to twenty minutes. Don't let this warm and meaningful time for conversation escape you.

On the other hand, a woman must not take her husband's sudden loss of sexual interest as a rejection of her. She needs to understand that the purely physical part of his sex drive rises after a period of physical abstinence and falls shortly after a climax. This does not mean that he no longer loves her, despite the fact that his sex drive has momentarily hit a low point.

Solving Sexual Problems

While sexual problems cause tension and unhappiness in many marriages, these difficulties can be solved more easily than one might think. In most cases it merely requires education. To deal with such problems, the couple willing to learn what they need to know and to practice it together will achieve fulfillment. Wives especially need to learn more about their sexuality. Before they can meet their husband's need for sex, they must know how to experience each of the stages I have described.

Many ask me, "How do we get educated?" It depends on how serious a problem you face. You may solve it by reading together any number of excellent books that discuss and illustrate sex for the married couple. Because it falls beyond the scope of this book, I have not attempted to go into detail on how to develop skills in lovemaking.

Read any sex manual with the goal of finding out what works for the two of you. Many such books will bombard you with all kinds of sexual procedures. But remember that some will work; some won't. No two couples respond in exactly the same manner. You must reach no "standard" other than feeling fulfilled, satisfied, and loved.

If you have a major sexual problem, you may need to visit a trained sex therapist. I have used sex therapy to help guide a few clients with sexual problems. But because each case I handle is of such an individual nature, I have not discussed therapeutic procedure here. If you feel your problem needs the individual attention of a sex therapist, it would be wise for you to first read a popular book offering solutions to common sexual problems. Then you can more intelligently explain your problems and identify a counselor who has the proper credentials to help you solve the problem.

One of the tragic ironies of my job appears when I counsel couples in their seventies for sexual incompatibility. Almost always they resolve their problem within a few weeks, and many experience sexual fulfillment for the first time after forty or fifty years of marriage. "What a difference this would have made in our marriage," they often report. While I am happy that they have finally resolved a longstanding and frustrating marital problem, I feel sad for the years they unnecessarily endured the guilt, anger, and depression that often accompany sexual incompatibility.

A Reluctant Husband

As I repeat throughout this book, not everyone has the typical needs of the "average" man or woman. An emotional need that I describe as being characteristic of most men can, in some cases, be a woman's most important emotional need. So, many times, it's actually the wife who craves sex, and it's the husband who is reluctant. In those cases, the three differences in sexuality between most men and women merit close analysis. When a husband is reluctant to make love, it's usually because one or more of these differences do not characterize the couple.

Generally I begin with an analysis of the first difference, sexual drive. Has the husband's level of testosterone dropped to a point where he no longer has a craving for sex? If so, a testosterone supplement can solve the problem. Many of my clients who are over fifty have chosen this solution to increase their sexual interest in their wife.

Another factor that affects sex drive for men is masturbation. Since most men experience a greatly reduced sex drive after an orgasm, men who masturbate frequently will probably show less interest in marital sex. That's one of the reasons I warn men to avoid any sexual experience that does not involve their wife—especially pornography. If a man's wife is his only source of sexual gratification, he is usually motivated to have sex with her as frequently as she wants.

The second difference, sexual awareness, can sometimes be the culprit. Because sex is so effortless for most young men, they will often assume that their sexual response will be available to them throughout life. Then, as they age, they find they have difficulty sustaining their arousal and become "impotent," which means they lose their erection while making love. Instead of having a predictably enjoyable experience, they suffer the indignity of sexual failure. This failure, in turn, creates an understandable sexual reluctance.

Medication to improve sexual performance is one solution to this problem. But another solution is to do what I recommend for most women.

Try different positions and sexual techniques until you find one that is predictably effective in triggering a sexual response.

The third difference, sexual motivation, can also play a role in a husband's sexual reluctance if his wife has been demanding, disrespectful, or angry. A fight can ruin some husbands' desire for sex, even when their sex drive is functioning normally. And many couples fight daily. These men may want sex for the same reason most women do—to have an intimate and emotionally bonding experience. But if their wife is demanding, disrespectful, or angry, they don't want emotional bonding. They want to run for cover.

An analysis of a husband's sexual reluctance may reveal problems with his sexual drive, sexual awareness, and/or sexual motivation. Once that analysis is completed, the solution to his problem will probably be identified. Then it is incumbent on a husband to implement the solution so that he can fulfill his wife's need for sex.

Meeting Each Other's Needs

As I said in chapter 1, I want to make husbands and wives aware of each other's five most important emotional needs and how to meet them. I have started the discussion of these basic needs with two that I believe are absolutely foundational to a good marriage: affection for her and sex for him.

You may have found some of what I've said in this chapter irritating or even disgusting. Perhaps I offended some wives by talking about their need to "learn" about their sexuality. I'm willing to take that risk, because the stakes are so high. As I counsel couple after couple, two basic problems surface repeatedly. You may think of them as embarrassing, galling, or infuriating, but here are the facts:

1. While probably more in touch with their own sexuality because it is such a basic male drive, many men lack skill in lovemaking because they fail to understand a woman's need for affection as part of the sexual process. When a man learns to be affectionate, his lovemaking will become very different. The man interested only in satisfying his hunger for sex molests his wife more than anything else, because his

technique is insensitive to her feelings. He uses his wife's body for his own pleasure, while she gets more and more infuriated.

2. Conversely, many women don't understand their own sexuality well enough to know how to enjoy meeting a husband's compelling need for sex. To satisfy her husband sexually, a wife must also feel satisfied. I try to encourage wives not only to make their bodies available to their husband on a more regular basis but also to commit themselves to learning to enjoy the sex relationship as much as their husband does.

The Marital Golden Rule

For the wife to enjoy sex, she will need help from her husband. If he does not communicate his care for her often and effectively, she will feel that he is insensitive and uncaring. This principle of reciprocity is applied throughout this book. You can't enjoy your end of a marriage if your spouse doesn't enjoy his or her end. If you care about your spouse, you don't use or deny your spouse out of selfishness or ignorance.

Almost all cultures and ages know the Golden Rule. Jesus Christ taught us: "Do to others as you would have them do to you" (Luke 6:31). As you think about the concepts presented so far and look ahead to the other eight needs, please consider this slight revision of the Golden Rule. I call it Harley's Second Law of Marriage:

Meet your spouse's needs as you would want your spouse to meet yours.

Questions for Her

1. On a scale of one to ten, with ten being "very satisfactory," how would you rate the five stages of your sexual response with your husband?
Willingness ____ Arousal ____ Plateau ____ Climax ____ Recovery ____
2. If you rated any of the five steps fairly low, what can you do to overcome the problem?

3. After reading this chapter, what did you learn about you and your husband that you did not already know?

Questions for Him

1. Do the three primary differences in sexuality between men and women apply to you and your wife? Have you addressed these differences to create a mutually fulfilling sexual experience?
2. Do you feel entitled to have sex with your wife because you have made a commitment to have an exclusive sexual relationship with her? Has that feeling of entitlement ever kept you from doing what it takes to motivate her to make love more often (to be more affectionate and make the experience more enjoyable for her)?
3. According to the author, a woman is aroused by her husband's affection, attentiveness, warmth, kindness, and tender sensitivity. Do you consistently try to develop and express these qualities? What do you think your wife would say in answer to this question?

To Consider Together

1. Discuss your answers to the previous questions with each other.
2. "I warn men to avoid any sexual experience that does not involve their wife—especially pornography" (p. 62). There are many reasons for this warning. Think of a few. Do you agree or disagree? Share with each other how you feel about this statement.
3. The workbook *Five Steps to Romantic Love* contains the "Sexual Experience Inventory," the "Strategy to Discover the Five Stages of Sexual Experience," the "Sexual Fulfillment Inventory," the "Strategy to Meet the Need for Sexual Fulfillment," and the "Sexual Fulfillment Worksheet." To help you communicate your sexual experiences to each other and create a mutually enjoyable sexual experience, you should complete these worksheets.

5

The Second Thing
She Can't Do
Without—Intimate
Conversation

When Julia and Nate dated, it was just one long conversation. On days when they could not be together in person, they would talk on the phone, sometimes for an hour or more. They rarely planned formal dates, because their real interest lay in seeing and talking with each other. Sometimes they got so busy talking, they forgot to do whatever they had planned for the evening.

But after their marriage, Julia and Nate found the number and quality of their conversations declining sharply. Both became involved in other things that took up more of their time. When they did have an opportunity to sit down and talk, Julia discovered Nate had less and less to say. When he came home from work, he generally buried his head in the newspaper, watched television, and went to bed early. It did not mean that Nate was uninterested in Julia or depressed about anything. He simply wanted to relax after a hard day at the office.

"Honey," Julia said one day, "I really miss our talks. I wish we could talk more the way we used to."

"Yeah," Nate replied, "I enjoyed those times too. What would you like to talk about?"

That comment did not score as a deposit in Julia's Love Bank. She didn't say it, but she thought, *If you don't know the answer to that question, then I guess we don't have anything to talk about.*

After that, Julia began to wonder why things had changed. Nate could still be talkative when he wanted to be—for example, with a group of people at a ball game. He seemed to reserve his silence for her alone, and she found it hard not to resent it.

Frequently Nate and Julia spent time with Tom and Kay, a couple their same age in the neighborhood. Julia noticed that Tom seemed to make a practice of directing his conversation to her and had no problem thinking of things to say.

Over a period of time, Julia found that getting together with Tom and Kay had become a high point of her week. She looked forward to those times when she could talk about the various things on her mind. Tom always listened attentively and did a great job of holding up his end of the conversation. As time went on, their friendship deepened. Whenever they were in large groups, at parties for example, Tom would pick her out to be with and talk to. He would sit with Julia at meetings and invite her to special events they found mutually interesting.

Julia eventually realized that her relationship with Tom had become more than a friendship for her. So, one day, she tentatively told him that she was falling in love with him.

"Julia," Tom replied, "I have been in love with you almost from the first time we met."

Within a few weeks Julia and Tom became deeply involved in an affair.

For some reason, Nate's attentiveness through conversation had fallen apart after the wedding and Julia's feeling of love for him fell apart along with it. Tom moved in to fill the need Nate was no longer meeting and now she was in love with him.

Why Won't My Husband Talk to Me?

A question I frequently hear from women is, "Why is it so difficult for my husband to have a simple conversation with me?" Part of the answer to their question is that men tend not to have as great a need for conversation as women. Most women enjoy conversation for its own sake. They will spend hours with each other on the telephone, while men rarely call each other just to chat and be brought up to date.

Why, then, do men find it so easy to talk to women about personal concerns when they are dating? One obvious reason is that the man wants to get to know the woman. First and foremost, he tries to understand her problems and how he can, or if he can, help her overcome them; he wants to know what will make her happy and fulfilled.

Her personal history is also important to him. He asks questions about her family, her childhood, her greatest achievements and disappointments, and her past romantic relationships.

In this same vein he wants to learn how to be attractive to her. Because he understands that she likes to be called, he promptly and regularly telephones whenever they cannot be together. This shows her how much he cares about her and thinks of her.

But after marriage he feels that he's learned enough about her and he's proven his care—by marrying her! Since his need for conversation is usually much less than hers, he doesn't see any purpose in continuing to have the long conversations they enjoyed while dating. He fails to understand that it was their intimate conversations that triggered her feeling of love for him. By removing intimate conversation from their daily lives, he removes one of his most important sources of love units into her Love Bank. He risks losing her love for him.

It Takes Time to Talk

A woman wants to be with a man who cares deeply about her and for her. When she perceives this kind of caring, she feels close to him, which is an essential ingredient in her willingness to make love with him. Since intimate conversation is one of the most important ways that a man communicates that care to a woman, intimate conversation and affection are inseparably entwined. So, just as affection should be a daily part of married life, intimate conversation should also continue *on a daily basis*. But how much time should be spent each day in intimate conversation?

More to the point, most men want to know the *minimum* amount of time his wife needs.

I studied this very question by investigating couples who were in love. How much time did they give each other? I studied couples who were dating, couples who had maintained romantic love while married, and couples having affairs. In all of these cases, I found that those who maintained their love for each other scheduled time to be together almost every day. While their daily time together varied, the time they spent each week was almost always over fifteen hours. During that time they had each other's undivided attention, and they used most of it to engage in intimate conversation.

Based on these findings, and overwhelming evidence I've acquired since then, I tell couples that if they want to maintain their love for each other, they should learn to do what those in love are doing—set aside at least fifteen hours a week for undivided attention, where one of the primary purposes is to engage in intimate conversation.

When they hear this advice for the first time, many men look at me as if they think I'm losing my mind, or they just laugh and say, "In other words, I need a thirty-six-hour day." I don't bat an eye but simply ask them how much time they spent giving their wives undivided attention during their courting days. Any bachelor who fails to devote something close to fifteen hours a week to his girlfriend faces the strong likelihood of losing her.

What happens on a typical date during courtship? A couple finds an activity that provides an excuse to get together. Usually they share a recreational activity, like playing tennis or going to a movie or out to dinner. But most of the time the activity is incidental. They *really* get together just to be with each other, and much of their time is spent showing each other affection and having enjoyable conversation.

The undivided attention they give each other on their dates makes deposits into each other's Love Bank accounts, but the deposits into his account in her Love Bank are massive. They're so massive that the affection and intimate conversation he gives her may be all it takes for the romantic love threshold to be breached and for her to fall in love.

Some couples, like Joyce and me, keep having dates throughout their marriage. They continue to give each other the same undivided attention that they gave each other before marriage. As a result, their love for each other is sustained for life. We're still in love after forty-eight years.

But other couples decide they don't have time for undivided attention after marriage. They feel, especially after children arrive, that there are more important things to do with their time. These couples lose their feeling of love for each other.

Without much time with their husband, women tend to lose the sense of intimacy they need so much, and their Love Bank is drained of funds. That loss greatly impacts their ability to enjoy sexual intimacy with their husband. Time and time again, wives have encouraged me to stick to my fifteen-hour minimum for undivided attention. They know it's necessary for a healthy marriage.

The Importance of Conversation

There are many reasons why effective conversation in marriage is absolutely essential to its success. But there are three that I believe are especially important.

First, conversation is an integral part of how all of the other important emotional needs are met. As I've already mentioned, the expression of affection is generally verbal, and sexual adjustment requires deep and sensitive communication. But consider for a moment the other emotional needs we will be discussing: recreational companionship, honesty and openness, physical attractiveness, financial support, domestic support, family commitment, and admiration. There isn't a single emotional need that can be met without requiring conversation in one way or another.

A second reason conversation is important in marriage is that it's necessary for everyday problem solving and conflict resolution. Marriage is a partnership that requires mutual agreement on a host of issues if it's to be successful. Conflicts over friends and relatives, financial planning, time management, child discipline, and many other common problems can be resolved only if couples are skilled in talking to each other. The more enjoyable and safe the conversation is, the more likely they will find mutually agreeable resolutions.

Most men understand these first two reasons for conversation. And they're usually willing to talk to their wife to try to address other emotional needs and resolve conflicts, particularly when the issue involves their need for sexual fulfillment.

But the third reason that conversation is important in marriage isn't understood as well by most men. We've already been discussing it in this chapter. Conversation itself is important because it meets a basic emotional need for most women. In other words, most women enjoy talking.

Not just any conversation makes enough Love Bank deposits to breach the romantic love threshold; it must be intimate conversation. A woman is very likely to fall in love with a man who is an expert at talking to her about her personal feelings, past experiences, present activities, and plans for the future. When she has an opportunity to express her concerns and consider her options, she can't resist him.

The first emotional need met in most affairs is intimate conversation. The wife whose husband won't talk may think that it's harmless to find a male friend to talk to her instead. As long as she remains faithful to her husband sexually, she feels that the "friendship" is safe and moral. Her problem is that by meeting her need for intimate conversation, her friend makes such large Love Bank deposits into his account that she becomes emotionally bonded to *him* instead of to her husband.

As she feels herself drifting into the arms of her friend, she makes an effort to become reunited with her husband. Deep down she knows that if she is to feel emotionally connected to him, he must talk to her.

"George, let's talk."

"What would you like to talk about?"

George's innocent inquiry misses the point and it upsets Mary. It shows how little he understands that conversation itself meets her emotional need. He might understand Mary's aggravation better if they had the following conversation.

"Mary, let's make love."

"Why, George? Are we ready to have children?"

Mary's response to George's question about sex helps us appreciate how inappropriate George's question about conversation appears to many women. It's not *what* they talk about that's important. It's *that* they talk.

Just as George finds sex enjoyable in its own right, Mary needs conversation. But just as it is with sex, there are ways to converse that make the experience more enjoyable. For most women, the more intimate the conversation, the better.

George sees conversation primarily as a means to an end and not an end in itself. So he talks to Mary only if there's a problem to be solved. If he wants to find out how the bank account got overdrawn, you can be sure he'll talk to Mary, but he's not likely to talk about how nice she looks today or if she's feeling better after having had a cold for a week. Women understand that conversation has practical purposes but they have a hard time explaining to their husband that they simply enjoy talking to him about almost anything, but especially about personal issues.

How are you feeling? What problems are you facing? How can I help you solve those problems? That's the kind of conversation that helps married couples stay in love with each other. Or it leads people into affairs when it's done outside of marriage and with someone of the opposite sex. It's intimate conversation.

Intimate Conversation and the Problem of Expressing Criticism

Charlotte came to work a little early so she could clear up some work left over from the day before. Her boss, Jack, thought that the bid on a project she had written needed to be improved, so she was rewriting it. Steve stopped at her desk with a cup of coffee for her—black, the way she liked it.

"Thanks. So you're here early too," she observed.

"Yeah, it gives me a chance to relax a little before hitting the trenches. How are you doing? I heard via the grapevine that Jack was pretty unreasonable yesterday."

"I can handle Jack," she responded. "What's really upset me this morning is my husband."

Charlotte and Steve are having an intimate conversation. He has shown an interest in how she feels, expresses his care for her (coffee), and supports her position even though it means being critical of her (and his) boss. But then she shifts the emphasis away from their boss and focuses attention on her husband as the greater source of her unhappiness.

I would warn Charlotte to avoid such conversation with Steve, since it could lead to an affair. She should have intimate conversation only with her husband, Bill. But I think you can understand how poorly motivated she would be to follow my advice to discuss her problems with him, when he turns out to be the biggest problem of all.

Intimate conversation focuses attention on what you're feeling, thinking, and doing. It's personal. Once in a while, Charlotte would tell Bill that unless he started paying more attention to her, she wouldn't be around to ignore. But he would brush her off, telling her that he didn't have time to hear her "bitching." That would usually lead to a fight, with each of them hurling insults at each other. Without a supportive partner willing to help solve their marital problems, intimate conversation is impossible. So Charlotte talks to Steve instead.

Of course Steve has a tremendous advantage over Bill in being able to talk intimately with Charlotte. She isn't being critical of him. She's being critical of Bill. So it's easy for him to talk to Charlotte about the problems she has with her husband. If it were about problems she was having with Steve, it would be an entirely different matter. The conversation would not be nearly as enjoyable.

When a couple begins an affair, they have very few negative reactions toward each other. So when they talk, they rarely criticize each other. Their criticism is directed mostly toward their spouses. It gives them the illusion that they are perfect for each other, and that adds greatly to their Love Bank deposits.

But ultimately, every couple, even those having an affair, experience disappointment. Emotional needs are not being met appropriately—or not at all. Decisions are made that fail to take the other person's feelings and interests into account. Offensive comments slip out. These and other mistakes create problems for the couple that must be solved, or they will lose their love for each other.

Before they have to face conflicts common in marriage, a couple having an affair think they love each other unconditionally. But when conflicts arise, as they always do, they don't handle them any better than they did in marriage, and they become disillusioned. "Maybe we're not soul mates after all."

The intimate conversation that's typical in most affairs does not focus attention on problems the two lovers have with each other. But intimate conversation in marriage *must* deal with those problems because spouses affect each other so much. In fact spouses have such a tremendous influence on each other that two of the best questions they can ask each other are, "What did I do to make you feel good today?" and, "What did I do to make you feel bad?"

If something I do affects my wife, Joyce, negatively, I need to know about it so I can eliminate that behavior and do something pleasing to her instead. Conversely, if I'm doing something right, I need to know that too so I can continue or even increase that behavior. Couples can't work too hard or too long at this process, because even doing something with the best intentions can backfire if they don't keep in touch this way.

What prevented Charlotte from having intimate conversation with her husband? What mistakes did they both make that could have led her into an affair? I call these common mistakes the *enemies of intimate conversation.* Not only do they prevent spouses from solving problems that they have with each other, they can also prevent spouses from talking to each other at all. And this is a major source of Love Bank withdrawals.

The Enemies of Intimate Conversation

Enemy #1: Making Demands

There's nothing wrong with asking for what you want from each other. In fact I've written this book to help you ask for and then get it from each other. But when your requests turn into demands, you've turned a corner that leads to Love Bank withdrawals.

Whenever you make a demand, you are telling your spouse you don't really care how he or she feels when fulfilling it. You want what you want, and that's all that matters. Of course you may have fifty reasons why it's just and proper for your spouse to give you what you want. But the bottom line is that demands give your spouse no right to refuse. They destroy intimate conversation and withdraw love units.

But they do more than that. Demands also make it *less* likely that you'll get what you want later. Even if you manage to force your spouse to obey your command this time, you can bet that he or she will be on guard next time and attack fire with fire. Not only are demands enemies of intimate conversation, they are also very foolish ways of trying to get what you may need, and may even deserve, in your marriage.

Charlotte had legitimate needs that her husband, Bill, should have met for her. But the way she went about trying to get his attention drove him away. Instead of encouraging him to address her complaints, she became controlling. She tried to force him to meet her needs by demanding that he comply. It didn't work for her and it won't work for you.

A better approach to any marital problem is to ask, "How would you feel about helping me with a problem I've been having?" It communicates care for your spouse, a willingness to negotiate, and an appeal to your spouse's care for you—essential elements of intimate conversation. Demands, on the other hand, communicate the opposite.

Enemy #2: Being Disrespectful

A sure way to end intimate conversation is to say something that can be construed as being disrespectful. Even something as simple as rolling your eyes in response to a spouse's comment can end what could have been a very enjoyable evening together. It's a lesson that some spouses never seem to learn.

Avoiding disrespect in marriage doesn't mean that you must agree with everything your spouse does or says. In fact, conflict is to be expected in even the most successful marriages. But the way you disagree should not be offensive.

"But what if I *don't* respect my spouse's opinion," I often hear. "What should I say then?"

My answer has emotional and logical implications: *Regardless of how you feel, don't say anything that's disrespectful.* It's an emotionally wise thing to do because disrespect makes massive Love Bank withdrawals and usually cripples intimate conversation. And it's a logical thing to do because disrespect prevents couples from finding mutually agreeable solutions to their problems. Instead of searching for common ground, the discussion degenerates into a fight or ends with the offended spouse walking away.

When Bill told Charlotte that he didn't have time to hear her "bitching," she immediately responded with emotional withdrawal and refused to sleep in the same bed with him that night. Often that's the effect that disrespect has on marriages.

But sometimes spouses express disrespect unintentionally. They think that their judgments simply reflect their honest opinion. If Charlotte had asked Bill for more attention, he might have responded, "You shouldn't depend on me so much." That's another way to be disrespectful because it's placing a value judgment on her request—she was wrong to have wanted more attention. If she had expressed offense at his comment, he might have made another disrespectful statement, "You're being too sensitive." Even though he might not think he was being disrespectful, their conversation would have suffered a fatal blow.

Since disrespect can be unintentional and poorly understood, if there's ever a question about what makes a comment disrespectful, I have a simple way of answering it. If your spouse considers what you say to be disrespectful, it is.

Enemy #3: Expressing Anger

As damaging as they are to intimate conversation, demands and disrespect can be innocent. Spouses don't necessarily want to hurt each other when they engage those enemies—it just turns out that way.

But expressions of anger are always *intended* to be hurtful. So when spouses are angry with each other, they should say absolutely nothing until they've had a chance to cool off, because whatever they say will be abusive—and insane. Yes, insane. Take it from me, a clinical psychologist, when people are angry, they are experiencing temporary insanity and should say nothing until their anger subsides.

Angry outbursts have no place in any area of your life, but they are especially destructive in marriage. Your marriage should be a relationship of mutual protection and care. But anger turns you into your spouse's biggest threat. Whatever you might think of saying to your spouse when you're angry is better left unsaid. If you ever get a chance to see a video recording of one of your angry outbursts, you'll definitely agree with me.

Enemy #4: Dwelling on Mistakes, Past or Present

Mistakes are common in life and they're especially common in marriage. Whenever we fail to take an opportunity to make our spouse happy, or if we do something to make our spouse unhappy, we've made a mistake. But mistakes may be difficult to prove. What one person calls a mistake might seem correct or at least justifiable from another's perspective.

An affair with Steve would be one of the biggest mistakes Charlotte could make. Bill would certainly regard it as a mistake, but she would be unlikely to see it that way while it's happening and she might not even see it that way after it's over. In fact she'd probably blame Bill for her affair.

If it's difficult to establish blame for something as obviously offensive as an affair, can you imagine how difficult it would be to do it for lesser offenses? And yet it's common for spouses to dwell on each other's mistakes and argue about who's to blame for their problems.

If Bill were to hammer Charlotte with constant reminders of how much suffering he went through because of her affair, and how difficult it is to forgive her, she wouldn't stick around very long for those conversations. And she might not even stay with him at all. He would be driving her away.

That's what happens when you dwell on each other's mistakes. You drive each other away emotionally if not physically.

There's nothing wrong with expressing the fact that your spouse did something that offended you. The enemy that I'm referring to here is "dwelling" on the mistake. If you keep bringing it up, repeating it again and again, it will destroy intimate conversation.

If my wife, Joyce, tells me that I've done something that annoys her or has offended her, I should accept her statement at face value. After all, she is the best judge of her own feelings. When she makes such a comment, she has revealed the impact of my behavior on her feelings. If I care for her feelings, I want her to help me learn how to behave in a way that meets her needs. But if after I accept her statements as true, she still dwells on my mistakes, it makes me feel defensive. Instead of wanting to solve the problem, I want to avoid further discussion of the issue. It's an enemy of intimate conversation.

Harley's Third Law of Marriage sums it up this way:

Caring partners converse in a caring way.

The Friends of Intimate Conversation

The four enemies I've just introduced to you discourage intimate conversation. Now I'd like to introduce four friends that encourage it. Two of them describe its content and two of them describe its rules of etiquette.

Friend #1: Conversing to Inform, Investigate, and Understand

One of the most valuable uses of marital conversation is to create emotional closeness. Nothing does that better than talking about each other in positive and encouraging ways. The more you learn about each other, and use that information to support each other, the more intimate your conversation becomes.

If you have a defensive relationship, where your conversation tends to be critical instead of supportive, you may deliberately give each other *misinformation*. You may *discourage investigation*. You may be *afraid to be understood* by your spouse. These common weaknesses lead to a serious and often disastrous failure to adjust to each other's needs. If you want a satisfying marriage, you must use your conversation to *inform*, *investigate*, and *understand* each other.

Inform each other of your personal feelings, interests, and activities. Answer every question honestly and respectfully. Provide information that your spouse wouldn't think to ask for. Keep calendars of your activities for the day and plans for your future and share them with each other. Tell your spouse your cell phone, social network, and email passwords, and don't erase anything until you have a chance to see each other's activity. Be completely transparent with each other—don't keep any secrets.

Investigate each other's personal feelings, interests, and activities without being demanding, disrespectful, or angry when you hear something that you feel should be changed. If you criticize or ridicule your spouse when he or she reveals personal information, it will be more difficult to express it in the future. Instead encourage each other to be open and vulnerable by being respectful and sensitive.

Understand each other's personal feelings, interests, and activities. What makes your spouse happy and sad and why does it have that effect? Learn about each other's "hot" and "cold" buttons, so you can bring the best out in each other and avoid the worst. One of the most important ways for you to care in marriage is to respond to that understanding with changes in your behavior that promote pleasure and avoid pain for each other.

Friend #2: Developing Interest in Each Other's Favorite Topics of Conversation

In my experience counseling couples, I have found that even the most introverted people become talkative when we discuss certain subjects. Women may notice that their quiet husband comes out of his shell when he's out with a few good male friends.

Once I counseled a woman who was about to divorce her husband because she could no longer accept his silence. But in my office, alone with me, he and I had no problem talking to each other. When his wife joined us, he became stone quiet. One problem was his wife's tendency to use all of the enemies of intimate conversation (demands, disrespect, anger, and dwelling on his mistakes) when she talked to him. But there was another problem. She never talked to him about topics that were of interest to him.

In my brief conversation with him, I was able to discover several topics that brought him out. Once these subjects were introduced while his wife was with us in the room, he talked just as much as she did.

After she stopped using the enemies of intimate conversation and started talking to him about his favorite topics, he was able to hold up his end of the conversation. Over time, the range of topics he could easily discuss broadened to include many that were of particular interest to her.

I encourage couples to learn about each other's favorite topics of conversation, even if some are not mutually interesting at first. Education tends to make most topics more interesting. The more you learn about something, the more curious you become.

Friend #3: Balancing the Conversation

Balance is the first rule of etiquette for intimate conversation. Much has been written about being a good listener, but being a good talker is just as important. That's the reason the first friend I mentioned was *informing and investigating*. You give information and receive information. Unless conversation is balanced in this way, it's not intimate conversation.

In the case I just mentioned, I had both husband and wife estimate the amount of time they spoke. Then in a ten-minute conversation, she was to allow him about five minutes. At first, she expected him to say nothing during his time. But once she stopped criticizing him, and they talked about subjects that interested him, he had no trouble filling his half of the ten minutes.

Some spouses ruin balance with the bad habit of interrupting. Before the other spouse can finish a thought, they break in with one of their own. Not only is this habit bad conversational etiquette, but it prevents those who are somewhat introverted from remembering where their thought was taking them. Interruptions can put an end to an otherwise enjoyable conversation.

Usually people who have trouble keeping a conversation going need a few seconds to begin what they have to say. I did a study once where I compared the conversational patters of socially outgoing people with those who were socially restrained. I found that when outgoing people talked with outgoing people, and restrained talked with restrained, the conversation tended to be balanced and they tended to say almost the same amount of words to each other. The problem came when the outgoing talked to the restrained. As you would expect, the outgoing dominated the conversation. Then I trained the outgoing people to avoid interrupting and give their restrained counterparts a few seconds to begin a sentence. With practice, the outgoing and restrained people learned to balance the conversation.

I used the results of that study to encourage outgoing spouses to give their restrained partner a little more time to get their thought pulled together. Sometimes I encouraged them to use two stopwatches to limit the time that each of them could speak (five minutes for each in a ten-minute conversation). This helps the outgoing spouse understand how much he or she tends to prevent the restrained spouse from speaking.

Those who monopolize conversation create an unwanted habit in their spouses—silence. Therefore, if you want a good conversation, be sensitive to each other's right to "have the floor." It may take your spouse two or three seconds to begin a sentence, but allow whatever time is necessary. Also remember to wait until your spouse completes a thought before commenting on it.

Friend #4: Giving Each Other Undivided Attention

One of the quickest ways for a husband to infuriate his wife is to carry on a conversation with her while watching football. She becomes upset because he is not paying attention to what she is saying. He's more interested in the football game. She's offended because he has broken the second rule of etiquette required for intimate conversation. It's *undivided attention*.

Of course, husbands break this rule for much less absorbing reasons than football. Many wives have complained to me that their husband doesn't listen to what they have to say. Some even fall off to sleep while their wife is talking.

Part of the reason that undivided attention is lacking in the conversation of so many couples is that the other friends of intimate conversation are missing. They are not talking about each other or about topics of mutual interest. And the conversation is not balanced. Only the wife is doing the talking.

But that said, undivided attention will probably require practice, especially by men. A man should look into his wife's eyes while they are talking to each other—a sure indicator that he is giving her his attention.

As I discussed earlier in this chapter, I recommend that each week every married couple set aside fifteen hours for the purpose of giving each other their undivided attention. When I ask couples to document this time, I want a daily estimate from him and a daily estimate from her. Almost inevitably, her estimate of time for undivided attention is less than his. That's because women are usually more aware than men of what undivided attention really means. A woman tends to give a more accurate estimate because it's her need for intimate conversation that he needs to meet.

How to Compensate for Careers Requiring Overnight Travel

If a husband's job takes him out of town, the telephone can help maintain a sense of communication and closeness. But even if he calls home every night, when he returns, it's quite common for his wife to need a day or two to reestablish the bonding to her husband she had before he left. Women married to men who travel often tell me how hard they find adjusting to their spouse's return. One said, "It takes a while for me to feel close enough to make love."

That's why I recommend that, on returning from a trip, a couple arrange for child care and spend at least four hours together simply to reconnect. The time should be spent being affectionate and talking to each other. Without that time together, it can take days before she feels close enough to make love—and by then he's off on another trip.

Many, perhaps most, of the couples I counsel have marital problems that are job related. Jobs that require a lot of travel, like sales, airline positions, and executive work, wreak havoc on marriages. The in-and-out pattern of the spouse on the move makes it difficult, if not impossible, for a woman to maintain a sense of oneness. When *both* spouses travel regularly, it becomes twice the challenge to remain emotionally bonded. That's why affairs are particularly common when a husband and wife are not always together overnight.

Conversation Tips for Husbands and Wives

As a caring husband, a man converses with his wife in a way that enables her to reveal her deepest feelings. Through conversation he learns to meet many of her needs. But the *conversation itself* meets one of her most important marital needs. She simply wants him to talk to her.

I will end this chapter with a list that summarizes the ways you can care for your spouse with intimate conversation. We've dealt with all of them. Now it's time to put them into action.

1. Remember how it was when you were dating. You both still need to exhibit that same intense interest in each other and in what you have to say, especially about your feelings.
2. A woman has a profound need to engage in conversation about her concerns and interests with someone who—in her view—cares deeply about her.
3. Men, if your job keeps you away from home overnight or for days on end, think about changing jobs. If you cannot, find ways to restore the intimacy of your marriage each time you return from an absence so that your wife can begin to feel comfortable with you

again. (If the wife does most of the traveling, the same principle applies.)

4. Get into the habit of spending fifteen hours each week alone with your spouse giving each other undivided attention. Spend much of this time in intimate conversation.

5. Remember, most women *fall in love* with men who set aside time to share conversation and affection with them. They *stay in love* with men who continue to meet those needs.

6. Financial considerations should not prevent you from meeting your wife's need for intimate conversation. If your job doesn't give you enough time to be alone to talk, it is ruining your marriage. Your job should serve your marriage, not vice versa.

7. Never make demands on each other.

8. Never be disrespectful to each other. Respect your spouse's feelings and opinions, especially when yours are different.

9. Never say anything to each other when you are angry.

10. Never remind each other of past mistakes or dwell on present mistakes.

11. Use your conversation to *inform*, *investigate*, and *understand* each other.

12. Develop interest in each other's favorite topics of conversation.

13. Learn to balance your conversation. Avoid interrupting each other and try to give each other the same amount of time to talk.

14. Give each other your undivided attention during conversation.

When a husband meets his wife's need for conversation, they come to understand each other more clearly and learn what it takes to meet other basic needs. This in turn enables you to make massive Love Bank deposits into each other's Love Bank, which creates and sustains your romantic love for each other. Intimate conversation makes you irresistible.

Questions for Him

1. Do you spend enough time talking to your wife about her personal concerns? Do you give her at least fifteen hours of your undivided attention each week? If not, why not?

2. Do you try to develop a better understanding of your wife's favorite topics of conversation? How can you improve?

3. Are you guilty of any "enemies of intimate conversation"? If so, how can you change?

Questions for Her

1. Do you miss the quality of conversation you had while you were dating? If so, what can you do to help restore it?

2. If you are separated overnight or for a few days, do you feel disconnected from your husband? Would a few hours of "reentry" help when you are first reunited?

3. What interests do you and your husband have in common? What can you do to develop your understanding of his favorite topics of conversation?

To Consider Together

1. Do the enemies of intimate conversation prevent you from talking to each other as often as you should? If so, what can you do to eliminate them?

2. Do the friends of intimate conversation dominate the way you talk to each other? If not, what can you do to bring them on board?

3. How can you rearrange your schedules to allow you to give each other fifteen hours a week of undivided attention? Would the time you currently spend doing something else be better spent with each other?

The Second Thing He Can't Do Without—Recreational Companionship

6

"Hi, Cindy, this is Alan."

"Hello! How nice of you to call." Her voice sounded warm and cheerful.

"I have tickets for the Bruins-Bears game at the Rose Bowl on Saturday. Would you like to go with me?"

"That sounds great! What time?"

They made the date, and Alan smiled after he hung up. He and Cindy had dated twice in the four weeks they had known each other. This would be the first "sports date," and he was pleased that she sounded so eager to go.

They had a great time at the game. Cindy seemed to understand enough about football to know what was happening, and they even discussed some of the plays afterward at the coffee shop.

That autumn they took in several more games in addition to a half dozen movies. Cindy's taste in films pleased Alan too, and the romance was progressing nicely. By midwinter Alan felt convinced he had found the right girl—at last. The weekend his car broke down doubly confirmed it in his mind. He called Cindy to explain.

"Honey, I'm sorry. My car won't run, and I've got to try to fix it this afternoon to have it for work on Monday."

"Oh, that's okay. Why don't I get my roommate to run me over and I'll give you a hand. I'll bring coffee and sandwiches."

The car repair turned into one of their best dates ever. Cindy handed Alan tools and generally made herself useful while they talked about some of the latest car models.

This girl, thought Alan, *is really special.*

They arranged their wedding for the first week in May. On their honeymoon they went to the mountains to do a little hiking together. The summer passed blissfully with some trips to the beach, and everything went very well—until football season. At the last minute, Cindy begged off on going with Alan to see UCLA play Arizona State. By the end of the season, the only other games she attended with him were Oregon State and the big one against University of Southern California. So one night at dinner, early in December, Alan brought this turn of events to Cindy's attention. "I thought you liked football," he complained.

"Oh, honey, I do. I guess I just don't enjoy it quite as much as you do. A couple of games during the season are enough for me," she replied.

"Oh," said Alan flatly, not sure how to handle this new and unexpected information.

"I've been meaning to ask you about something," she continued. "The county art museum has a special exhibit of Spanish Renaissance painters this month. Would you go with me?"

"Yeah, sure, I guess so," Alan replied.

Over the next year, Alan discovered that the things he liked to do and the things Cindy *really* liked to do had little in common. Her interest in cars had evaporated practically overnight, and he felt lucky to get her to even one football game. Meanwhile, she insisted that he take her to more art museums and an occasional concert or opera. Alan balked at all this culture, and gradually they arrived at the point where they rarely did much together except go out to dinner once in a while.

At the end of two years of marriage, they had an agreement that he would spend an evening or an afternoon each week with his friends, and she would do the same with her friends. Alan would have preferred to spend more "fun" time with Cindy, but she seemed quite content with the arrangement.

Hurt and bewildered, Alan often asked himself, *I wonder what made her change?*

How Important Is Recreational Compatibility?

In counseling sessions, I have heard many variations of the saga of Cindy and Alan. Of course Cindy never really "changed." It is not uncommon for women, when they are single, to join men in pursuing their interests. They find themselves hunting, fishing, playing football, and watching movies they would never have chosen on their own. After marriage, wives may try to interest their husband in activities more to their own liking. If their attempts fail, they may encourage their husband to continue his recreational activities without them.

That's a dangerous choice, though, because men place surprising importance on recreational activities. When dating, recreational compatibility is usually a crucial criterion for men in selecting a wife, and they assume that their bride will become their lifelong recreational companion. In most cases, her interest in his favorite activities helps make enough Love Bank deposits to seal the marriage deal.

So when a wife announces after marriage that she's no longer interested in joining him in his favorite activities and that he should enjoy them with his friends instead, it usually comes as a shock. It also eliminates one of the most important ways that she makes Love Bank deposits.

Most men treasure the time they spend recreationally. They plan for it, look forward to it, and will often spend quite a bit of money making it especially enjoyable. The TV stereotypes showing husbands out with the boys on fishing trips saying, "It doesn't get any better than this," make that point. But my counseling files prove that it *can* get a lot better than that if a husband's favorite recreational companion is his wife. In fact, among the five basic male needs, *spending recreational time with his wife is ranked second only to sex for the typical husband.* It's so important that I consider it to be a need that *must* be met to sustain his feeling of love in marriage.

People may challenge my claim, saying they know any number of happily married couples whose recreational interests are totally different. But these people do not necessarily know the couples in their most honest moments. I have counseled married couples who maintain an excellent image right up to the moment of divorce. They successfully hide their deepest needs from themselves and others until it is too late.

Sometimes recreational tastes overshadow deep personal needs. By nature men and women seem to have divergent tastes when it comes to having fun. Many men enjoy recreational activities that involve more risk, more adventure, and more violence than women enjoy. Typically men pursue such sports as football, boxing, hunting, fishing, hang gliding, scuba diving, snowmobiling, and skydiving. They tend to prefer movies with sex and violence and don't mind sweat, dirt, body odor, or belching during a recreational activity. Most women find all of this terribly unpleasant and tasteless.

Women prefer to engage in quieter activities, such as romantic movies, cultural events, going out to lunch or dinner, dancing, and the all-time favorite, shopping. They tend to put less emphasis on the activity itself and more emphasis on the social interaction. Whom they are with is usually more important than what they are doing. For most women, a good conversation can be a recreational event.

The classic struggle finds the woman trying to "clean up the man's act," making him shave, dress more neatly, talk more gently, and so on. When she moves in on his recreational life, he may conclude she wants to spoil one of the only things that keep him going in life. He still loves her, but she begins to cramp his style. To avoid that, he spends an increasing amount of time with men only. This allows him to do what he enjoys most without restraint. But it also means that his most enjoyable activities are done without his wife present. And an opportunity for her to make huge Love Bank deposits is lost.

Growing Apart

In our opening story, Alan was disappointed and wondering why Cindy had changed. In some marriages, a man like Alan would just trudge off alone to watch his Bruin gridders and make the best of it. But what happened to Alan is all too common. He joined a softball league with some of his buddies, where he met Hillary, who just loves sports of all kinds. They had a cup of coffee as they shared baseball trivia, and before you knew it, they became good friends. (After all, softball leagues last for months.)

If Alan doesn't watch it, he will find himself in an affair with Hillary, who promises to meet all those recreational needs Alan expects Cindy to meet. If the story plays out to its ironic end, Alan will divorce Cindy to marry Hillary and—you guessed it—*she* will suddenly decide concerts, or maybe croquet matches, are more fun than baseball or football. I have seen this exact irony come back to haunt men who thought an affair, divorce, and remarriage would solve their problems.

I must emphasize that men like Alan don't usually wander into an affair out of anger or revenge. Alan felt hurt by Cindy's change of behavior but he didn't begrudge her the right to revert to her real interests. The danger in all of this lies in the two of them simply continuing to grow farther and farther apart. That common pattern at its worst can lead to an affair and divorce; the wise couple will avoid this trend in their marriage or correct it as soon as it begins.

It Happened to Me Too

I understand the confusion Alan and other husbands like him face when their wife starts to retreat from recreational activities they once enjoyed together. I've been there too. For example, when I was younger, I loved to play chess. I started at age four and eventually became president of the university club, where I was first board.

After I married, I gave up chess tournaments because Joyce didn't play and had no interest in learning. Chess is an extremely time-consuming game, and as much as I loved it, I decided we could better spend our recreational time doing something we both enjoyed. I thought we would both enjoy tennis, since we had spent countless hours playing during courtship days. But during the first year of marriage, Joyce announced, "Bill, I don't really enjoy tennis that much anymore. I think I would prefer other ways of spending time together."

Joyce's turnaround on tennis came as a complete surprise to me. We had dated for six years before we married, and I thought she had enjoyed tennis as much as I did. I didn't realize that she played it just to be with me. But after we were married, she reasoned, we'd be together without having to do things that she didn't enjoy. So, early in our marriage, she did the right thing. She let me know that tennis wasn't her favorite activity and that she'd rather we do something else together.

This was a very important choice-point in our marriage. I could have done what many spouses do—continue to play tennis with someone else. At the time, Joyce would probably have gone along with that solution, as long as my new partner was my friend Steve.

But I didn't make that decision. Instead, I chose a different path. I forgot about tennis and found a new activity that Joyce and I would enjoy together. We switched from tennis to volleyball and played on the same team. And we expanded our interests in movies, plays, concerts, dining out, exercising, sightseeing, and enjoying nature.

Because we stayed together in pursuit of recreation, today we spend almost all our recreational time with each other. The outcome could have been quite different if I had stuck to tennis and chess and let Joyce go her way. We would have grown apart, each experiencing our most enjoyable moments of fun and relaxation without the other.

When I counsel married couples, I can't emphasize too strongly what a mistake it can be for spouses to have independent recreational activities. Instead of making steady deposits in each other's Love Bank by having fun together, the couple with separate recreational interests misses a golden opportunity. They spend some of their most enjoyable moments in the company of *someone else,* with the distinct possibility of building a Love Bank account with that person. When spouses are not each other's favorite recreational companion, not only do they risk losing their love for each other, but they also risk falling in love with whoever turns out to be their companion, if it's someone of the opposite sex.

If you want to have a fulfilling marriage, your favorite recreational companion *must* be your spouse.

How to Find Mutual Recreational Interests

When I explain the importance of mutual recreational interests to couples in my office, some have no problem discovering things to do together. Others, however, are at a total loss. They are just too different, they claim. And "besides *he* simply won't give up his golf." Or "*she* absolutely must continue her book club on Tuesday afternoons."

In response to their pessimistic attitude, I say, "Imagine that around each of you is drawn an invisible circle encompassing all your recreational interests and sources of enjoyment. There are thousands of them—some you know about, and some have yet to be discovered. Within each of your circles there are hundreds of recreational interests that overlap—you both enjoy doing them. Again, you may vaguely know about some of them, but almost all are still a mystery. From the hundreds of overlapping interests, you need to find only a few because you won't have time for all of them. Once you find, say, five or ten activities that you both enjoy doing together, and spend all of your recreational time together, you'll become each other's favorite recreational companion."

To discover these overlapping recreational interests, I encourage the couple to complete my Recreational Enjoyment Inventory (a copy can be found in appendix C). It's a list of 125 recreational activities with space to indicate how much a husband or wife likes or dislikes each one. Ratings are from -3 (very unpleasant) to +3 (very enjoyable). Couples can add activities to the list that are not already included and rate them as well. When the list is completed, it may include as many as 200 activities, each with an enjoyment rating by both husband and wife, with the activities that have been rated enjoyable (at least +2) by *both* husband and wife identified. This exercise usually produces a list of ten or fifteen activities both spouses can enjoy together. In the weeks to come I ask them to schedule each of these activities into their recreational time. Some of these choices will be things he may like a bit more than she does, and vice versa, but in every case, they will both be depositing love units as they spend recreational time together. Eventually, they settle on about five activities that they both enjoy most.

No one can do *everything* he or she would like in life. There's just not enough time. So every person's recreational time amounts to making choices among enjoyable activities. Why not select those activities you both enjoy and can do together?

A Husband's Favorite Recreational Companion

When a couple draws up their master list of mutually enjoyable activities, there are many surprises. Some are activities that neither have ever experienced before. They simply sounded like they might be enjoyable. Other surprises are activities that the couple didn't realize were mutually enjoyable. They both thought the other disliked doing them.

But there's another surprise that couples often face: finding that something they are already doing together is unpleasant for one of them. What are they to do with that activity?

After Joyce and I were married, she knew what to do with tennis—toss it out of our lives. But there are many wives who would not have made that decision. They would have gone on playing tennis with their husbands, sacrificing their own pleasure so that their husband would be happy. In other words, deposits into his Love Bank would have created withdrawals in hers.

A husband will often try to do the same thing. He'll do something with his wife that only she enjoys. In those situations, he's not engaged in his favorite recreational activity, and his wife is not his favorite recreational companion. Some other activity is his favorite, and the one who enjoys it with him becomes his favorite recreational companion. If that person is a woman, his marriage is at risk. But even if his companion is man, his wife is missing a great opportunity to make massive Love Bank deposits.

When I counsel a couple who have not yet learned how to be each other's favorite recreational companions, I give them a radical assignment:

> *Engage in only those recreational activities*
> *that you and your spouse can enjoy together.*

I explain that they can eventually participate in activities apart from each other. But until they become each other's favorite recreational companion, they must spend all of their leisure time together.

My assignment is tough because it rules out some activities that a couple may currently be doing together and it also rules out *all* recreational activities that they are doing apart that only one of them enjoys. Despite the difficulty, though, I insist on this rule for couples who have not yet learned to enjoy recreational activities together.

You can probably imagine the reaction of some. They are appalled that I would even suggest such a thing! It means, for example, that a husband might have to give up *Monday Night Football* if his wife doesn't enjoy it with him. Men who thought I was trying to help them out by encouraging their wife to join them in their favorite activities are faced with the prospect of abandoning these activities entirely. I'll admit I've lost the faith of a few spouses on this one. Many have felt I've gone too far.

But once you think it through, you have to agree with me, at least on principle. If you were to find recreational activities that both you and your spouse could enjoy together, just as much as you enjoy your favorite activities now, it would definitely improve your feelings for each other. And that's the goal I'm after. What's more important, the quality of your marriage or *Monday Night Football*? In some cases, that's the choice you have.

This assignment of engaging in only mutually appealing activities is not a summons to misery and deprivation, though. For me, it simply means that I should consider Joyce's feelings when selecting a recreational activity among those I already enjoy. Why should I gain at her expense when we can gain together?

There are a host of reasons that spouses should discover recreational activities they can enjoy together. For one, it reflects the care both spouses should have for each other. If one spouse sacrifices his or her enjoyment, it means the other is willing to gain at the spouse's expense. Whenever a sacrifice is made in marriage to please one's spouse, at that moment, one spouse doesn't care how the other spouse feels.

A second very important reason to discover those activities is that they stand up over time. Whatever it is that both you and your spouse enjoy together, you are very likely to do again. Do you want more affection? Express affection toward each other in a mutually enjoyable way. Do you want to make love more often? Make love to each other in a mutually enjoyable way. Do you want more intimate conversation? Talk intimately with each other in a mutually enjoyable way. And when it comes to recreational companionship, if you want to spend more of your leisure time together, make sure that you and your spouse enjoy the type of activity and the way you engage in that activity.

A third important reason to become each other's favorite recreational companion is it ensures deposits into each other's Love Bank—especially his. Some of my best feelings occur when I am engaged in a recreational activity. If I share it with Joyce, I associate those good feelings with *her*, which sustains my love for her. If I share it with another woman, I lose an opportunity to sustain my love for Joyce and risk developing love for that woman.

Many spouses, particularly husbands, find my assignment hard to put into practice. Just the thought of giving up their favorite activities, like hunting or football, causes depression to set in for some men. I can understand, because men need recreation in their life to keep going. They use leisure-time activities to recharge themselves. Then some marriage counselor comes along and tells them they can't do the very things that help keep them productive.

Still, I encourage such men to try my plan for just a few months, reminding them that I have not told them to give up recreational pleasures. I simply advise them to include their wife and choose activities they both enjoy. It's not a matter of giving up all the pleasures of life. Instead, a man must simply replace his old pastimes with some he can share with his spouse or make her a part of the ones he already enjoys.

In making the changes, a wife should be alert to the possibility that breaking a recreational habit can put some men into a state of withdrawal. He may miss it terribly at first. She may wonder if she's made a great mistake. She didn't mean to force herself on him, although she wants his companionship too. Halfway through their first activity together, she may want to tell him to return to an activity he's left, because she feels guilty for taking him away from something she knows he truly enjoys and deserves.

But eventually he will come to enjoy mutually appealing activities even more than those he could not share with his wife. This is because she has an easier time meeting some of his other basic emotional needs, such as sexual fulfillment, when she becomes his favorite recreational companion.

If, for one or both of you, an activity fails to be enjoyable after the first time or two, don't give up. Take the time required to gain some skill. Suppose a wife begins to take up skiing to please her husband. She needs time to build up the muscles required and learn the techniques that make her proficient. If he pushes her too fast, she may come to resent it and will quickly turn away from the sport. But if he's patient, she might find it very enjoyable.

However, if she tries skiing, gains some proficiency, then still dislikes it, the wife should have the freedom to tell her husband, "I've tried it. I still don't like it. Let's try something else."

Give yourselves time to adjust and to try new pastimes. You may have some difficulty accommodating these changes but you'll find the rewards for your marriage well worth the effort. In my counseling experiences I've found that couples who limit their recreational activities to those they do together make tremendous gains in compatibility. They also deposit scores of love units in each other's Love Bank.

Recreational Activities Included in Time for Undivided Attention

In the last chapter, I encouraged you to spend a minimum of fifteen hours a week giving each other undivided attention. The context of that recommendation was intimate conversation, so you may have been left with the impression that you should talk intimately to each other for fifteen hours each week. But talking isn't the only way to provide undivided attention. In fact the intimacy that results from undivided attention is usually achieved when a combination of four emotional needs are met—the top two emotional needs of most women, affection and intimate conversation, and the top two emotional needs of most men, sexual fulfillment and recreational companionship.

It should not be surprising that women define a romantic experience differently than men. For most women, a romantic evening meets her emotional needs for affection and intimate conversation—an evening of dinner, dancing, and a walk in the moonlight filled with expressions of love and stimulating conversation. Men, on the other hand, find romance in sexual fulfillment and recreational companionship—watching football on TV with sex during halftime!

Neither perspective on romance works very well for the opposite sex. So prior to marriage, most men and women combine all four needs into a romantic experience. That way, the needs of both men and women are met.

But after marriage, spouses get lazy and want to take shortcuts. Women find time for affection and intimate conversation but are too busy or too tired for sexual fulfillment or recreational companionship. On the other hand, men can drop almost anything for sexual fulfillment and recreational companionship but can't fit affection or intimate conversation into their busy schedules.

Don't make this mistake in your marriage. You both have intimate emotional needs that should be met by each other. But they're different, and you will be tempted to overlook your spouse's needs. By meeting all four of these needs in a single date, you will have an experience that both of you will consider romantic and you will be making massive Love Bank deposits as well.

With undivided attention in mind, you'll find that some recreational activities cannot be considered part of your fifteen hours. That's not to say you shouldn't engage in these other activities together. It's just that when considering what to do during your time for undivided attention, make sure that the activity doesn't distract you from each other. For example, if you focus most of your attention on a movie or a television show, that activity should not be considered part of your time for undivided attention. But if during the show, you are expressing affection to each other and your focus of attention is primarily on each other, then it counts. Any recreational activity that allows for affection, intimate conversation, and even sexual fulfillment while engaged in the activity is a good candidate.

Dancing, card games, hiking, boating, and even working out at the gym together have been favorites of couples who want a recreational activity that provides an opportunity for undivided attention. But don't include friends with any of those activities. They'll distract you from each other. You should have as much privacy as possible during your fifteen hours.

If you are to be each other's favorite recreational companion, there will be many activities you both enjoy that do not lend themselves well to undivided attention. As I already mentioned, you should engage in those activities as well, but don't let them, or anything else, crowd out your fifteen hours together.

My assignment to engage only in activities you can enjoy together as recreational companions is not unbearably painful or unrealistic. In fact, it's what you probably did when you first fell in love with each other. It invites both of you to a new level of intimacy and enjoyment of each other. Harley's Fourth Law of Marriage puts it this way:

> *The couple that plays together stays together.*

Questions for Her

1. Are you your husband's favorite recreational companion? If not, why not?
2. Are you reluctant to encourage your husband to suspend some of his recreational activities until you become his favorite recreational companion? If so, what would help you overcome that reluctance?
3. Does your husband join you in your favorite recreational activities? Are you willing to suspend those activities that he does not find enjoyable so that you can search for mutually enjoyable activities? Do you think he would be willing to do the same?

Questions for Him

1. Would you like your wife to become your favorite recreational companion? If not, why not?
2. Do you value your leisure time? If so, would having your wife join you make it more relaxing or less relaxing for you? If less relaxing, what could she do to make it more relaxing?
3. Does your wife join you in your favorite recreational activities? Are you willing to suspend those activities that she does not find enjoyable so that you can search for mutually enjoyable activities? Do you think she would be willing to do the same?

To Consider Together

1. Use the form Recreational Enjoyment Inventory, found in appendix C, to help you discover mutually appealing activities.
2. After identifying activities you both enjoy, schedule time to try each of them. Narrow them down to five or ten that you enjoy the most.
3. Try my "radical assignment": engage in only those recreational activities that you and your spouse can enjoy together until you become each other's favorite recreational companion.
4. In planning your fifteen hours for undivided attention, try to meet all four of the intimate emotional needs each time you have a date: affection, sexual fulfillment, intimate conversation, and recreational companionship. You'll find that each date will require about three or four hours—just as when you were dating each other.

7

She Needs to Trust Him Totally— Honesty and Openness

Nicole felt both perplexed and enchanted by Ted's mystique. She had never met a more private man, and he often evaded her questions. Near the end of a date, she might ask him where he was going or what he was planning to do. He would just wink, smile knowingly, and say, "I'll call you tomorrow."

Ted's behavior seemed a bit odd, but Nicole told herself that everybody has a right to privacy. Certainly Ted had a right to keep *some* things to himself.

Truth be told, Ted had several things he kept to himself—specifically other girlfriends he did not want Nicole to know about. When he couldn't conveniently evade her questions, he took pains to mislead her by telling her about nonexistent projects he had to complete at work. His true projects were dates with other women. Sometimes Nicole suspected him of seeing someone else, but he made such a big thing out of his right to privacy that she felt guilty whenever she questioned his honesty.

Besides, Ted had a lot of the other things Nicole wanted in a man. He was affectionate and charming. Other women cast envious looks when she walked into a party with such a tall, good-looking man. To ice the cake, he had an excellent income and spent money on her generously. When Ted proposed, all these pluses far outweighed his "I need my privacy" minus.

He'll tell me everything after we're married, Nicole thought.

As it turned out, Ted's behavior did not change after the wedding. In fact it seemed to become a bigger problem, because now that they lived together, Ted had more occasions than ever to be secretive.

Interestingly enough, all this need for privacy did not mean Ted was seeing another woman. Once he made the marriage commitment, he dropped his other girlfriends to "settle down." But he still reserved the "right" to get home from work when he felt like it. Since his job involved an irregular schedule, Nicole could seldom plan much of anything. Ted would call but would only say, "I'll be late—maybe by six thirty. I'm not sure." Nicole learned quickly that she was part of the "keep dinner warm in the oven" brigade. Once he did get home, Ted had none of the charm that dazzled her during courtship.

He had little to say when it came down to making plans. "Can I invite the Morgans for dinner Saturday night?" Nicole would ask.

"Not sure," Ted would reply. "I'll have to see—it's a busy week."

And so it went—from frustration to depression for Nicole. Ted remained faithful enough and he really had nothing to hide. For some reason, however—known only to him—he didn't want to share with Nicole what he was doing or thinking.

"At the wedding, our pastor said in marriage two become one," Nicole told her friend Meg. "But Ted and I really can't be one if he won't share his thoughts with me. I've asked if he would go with me to talk with our pastor, but he won't hear of it and he doesn't want me to go alone. He tells me people at church will find out and misunderstand. I wonder if he's had an affair."

Her Sense of Security

Nicole and Ted are headed for trouble unless he realizes he has to change. If Ted insists on going on with his mysterious routine, he will become increasingly frustrating to his wife, and this will slowly empty most of his Love Bank account. When it eventually drifts into negative territory, Nicole will become a vulnerable target for a man who knows how to make her feel secure with honesty and openness.

A sense of security is the bright golden thread woven through all of a woman's five basic needs. If a husband does not maintain honest and open communication with his wife, he undermines her trust and eventually destroys her sense of security.

To feel secure, a wife must trust her husband to give her accurate information about his past, the present, and the future. What has he done? What is he thinking or doing right now? What plans does he have? If she can't trust the signals he sends (or if, as in the case of Ted, he refuses to send any signals), she has no foundation on which to build a solid relationship. Instead of adjusting to him, she always feels off balance; instead of growing *with* him, she grows *away* from him.

The wife who can't trust her husband to give her the information she needs also lacks a means of negotiating with him. Negotiation between a husband and wife is an essential building block to the success of any marriage, but without honesty and openness a couple can resolve or decide very little.

Withholding information in marriage is bad enough. But when a spouse provides misleading or downright false information, it's a disaster. I cover the topic of dishonesty in chapter 6 of my book *Love Busters,* because it's one of the six most destructive habits a spouse can have in marriage. However, in this chapter, I will focus attention only on Ted's problem. He's not necessarily being dishonest—he's simply keeping his thoughts, activities, and plans to himself. He's failing to meet Nicole's need for honesty and openness.

Being Open

I tell couples I counsel that transparency is one of the most important qualities in a successful marriage. Nothing should be hidden from each other. Your spouse should know you better than anyone else does. But sadly, within a few short counseling sessions, I often know more about each spouse than they do about each other. I'm not clairvoyant or particularly sensitive to understanding people, but when I ask them questions, they both give me honest answers. They know they need help and they also know that the more information they provide, the more helpful I will be to them.

As each spouse "comes clean" with me, I get a clearer picture of both of them than they have ever had of each other. For years they have wandered around blindly in the smokescreens each has laid down for the other. When they talk to me, they have no need for a smokescreen, and the real problem or issue starts to emerge.

In most cases, it isn't the wife who does most of the hiding—it's the husband. She's the one who usually asks him, "What are you thinking?" and "How are you feeling?" and "What are you planning?"

Nicole asked Ted these questions many times, without getting any satisfactory responses. In fact, he usually made a joke of it. "Are you a reporter? Are you writing a book?" he would ask disrespectfully.

The result was that Nicole's emotional need for honesty and openness was unmet. But almost equally important, she wasn't able to grow in her understanding of Ted. After five years of marriage, she hardly knew him.

Privacy

Many people ask me, "When you say I have to be honest and open with my spouse, aren't you taking away all my privacy?" If by *privacy* this person means keeping part of himself or herself hidden, I hold firmly to my conviction that this word has no place in a husband and wife's relationship. Many—colleagues and clients alike—disagree, but I have seen too many marital disasters follow the compromise of my principle. Although you may find it threatening to think your spouse might have the right to read your email or go through your purse, I believe this kind of openness is indispensable for a healthy marriage.

When I "protect my privacy," it makes me less transparent to my wife. Joyce is the one person who needs to know me best, and I need to provide her with all the information—including the warts. Not only must I answer her questions truthfully but I must avoid "lies of silence" and readily volunteer information as well. In other words, I must share myself with her in every way possible.

The Policy of Radical Honesty

There are three very important reasons honesty and openness are essential in marriage. First, they provide a clear roadmap for marital adjustment. A husband and wife who are honest and open with each other can identify their problems very quickly and, if they know how to negotiate, dispose of them very swiftly. A lack of transparency covers up both the problems themselves and the solutions to those problems. The more facts you have, the better you'll understand each other. And the more you understand each other, the more likely it is that you'll come up with solutions to your problems.

The second reason for honesty and openness in marriage is that dishonesty, or covering the truth in some way, is painfully offensive. That offense causes such massive Love Bank withdrawals that I include it as one of the six major Love Busters. As I mentioned earlier in this chapter, I discuss dishonesty, and how to overcome it, in my book *Love Busters*.

But the third reason radical honesty is essential in marriage is the topic of this chapter—it meets an important emotional need. For many, especially women, honesty and openness deposit so many love units that they fall in love with the person who's radically honest with them. They need a clear and unobstructed view into the mind of the one they love.

Since the need for honesty and openness in marriage is so important to most women, I've given couples a rule that explains how far a husband (and wife) should go in revealing himself. I call it the Policy of Radical Honesty:

> *Reveal to your spouse as much information about yourself as you know—your thoughts, feelings, habits, likes, dislikes, past history, daily activities, and future plans.*

To make it clearer to you, and easier to understand, I'll break the policy down into four parts:

1. *Emotional honesty.* Reveal your thoughts, feelings, likes and dislikes. In other words, reveal your emotional reactions—both positive and

negative—to the events of your life, particularly to your spouse's behavior.

2. *Historical honesty.* Reveal information about your personal history, particularly events that demonstrate personal weakness or failure.

3. *Current honesty.* Reveal information about the events of your day. Provide your spouse with a calendar of your activities, with special emphasis on those that may affect him or her.

4. *Future honesty.* Reveal your thoughts and plans regarding future activities and objectives.

Let's take a careful look at each of the four parts of the Policy of Radical Honesty.

Emotional Honesty

Most couples do their best to make each other happy. But their efforts, however sincere, are often misdirected. They aim at the wrong target.

Imagine a man who buys his wife flowers every night on the way home from work. What a wonderful thing to do—except that his wife is allergic to them. Because she appreciates the gesture, though, she never mentions her allergies but just sniffles in silence. Soon, however, she begins to dread the thought of her husband coming home with those terrible flowers. Meanwhile, he's getting bored with the marriage because she is always feeling lousy and never has energy to do anything. But of course he won't tell her that.

This couple's marriage is in trouble, not because of any lack of effort, but because of their ignorance—ignorance caused by a lack of honesty. He thinks he's doing a good thing by bringing home flowers but he doesn't realize that the flowers are the cause of his wife's malaise. Let's say that, in his effort to show even more love for her, he brings home more and more flowers. Ultimately she's collapsed on the couch, gasping for breath, surrounded by flowers, while he wonders what went wrong.

Of course, this is a preposterous story, but it portrays the way many couples misfire in their attempts to please each other. Their lack of honesty and openness keeps them from correcting their real problems.

Some people, like Ted in our opening scenario, find it difficult to express their emotional reactions, particularly the negative ones. But negative feelings serve a valuable purpose in a marriage. They are a signal that something is wrong. If you successfully steer clear of the enemies of intimate conversation—demands, disrespect, and anger—your expression of negative feelings can alert both you and your spouse to an adjustment that must be made.

Emotional Honesty

Reveal your emotional reactions—both positive and negative—to the events of your life, particularly to your spouse's behavior.

Honesty and openness enable a couple to make appropriate adjustments to each other. And adjustment is what a good marriage is all about. The circumstances that led you into your blissful union will certainly change, if they haven't already, and you need to learn to roll with the tide. Both of you are growing and changing with each new day and you must constantly adjust to each other's changes. But how can you know how to adjust if you're not receiving accurate information about these changes? You'd be flying blind, like a pilot whose instrument panel has shorted out.

You need accurate data from each other. Without this, unhappy situations can go on and on—like the flowers piling up in the allergic woman's home. But the expression of your deepest feelings does more than help make correct adjustments to each other. It makes Love Bank deposits. Nicole *needed* Ted to express his feelings to her. It helped her become emotionally bonded to him—two becoming one. His failure to express his deepest thoughts and feelings made her feel locked out of his life.

Historical Honesty

Should your skeletons stay in the closet? Some say yes. Lock the door, hide the key, leave well enough alone. Communicate your past misdeeds only on a need-to-know basis.

But your spouse has a right to know, and needs to know, all about your past. Whatever embarrassing experiences or serious mistakes are in your past, you should come clean with your spouse in the present.

Historical Honesty
Reveal information about your personal history, particularly events that demonstrate personal weakness or failure.

Your personal history holds significant information about you—information about your strengths and weaknesses. If your spouse is to make appropriate adjustments, he or she should understand both your good and bad experiences to know when you can be relied on or when you might need help.

A man who has had an affair in the past is particularly vulnerable to another one. If a woman has been chemically dependent in the past, she'll be susceptible to drug or alcohol abuse in the future. If you express your past mistakes openly, your spouse can understand your weaknesses, and together you can avoid conditions that tend to create problems for you.

No area of your life should be kept secret. All of your spouse's questions should be answered fully and completely. Periods of poor adjustment in your past should be given special attention, because problems of the past are commonly problems of the future.

Not only should you explain your past to your spouse, but you should also encourage your spouse to gather information from those who knew you before you met. Talk with several significant people from each other's past. It can be a very helpful eye-opener!

I also encourage you to reveal to each other all romantic relationships you've had in the past. Names should be included along with a description of what happened.

"But if I tell my wife what I've done, she'll never trust me again."

"If my husband finds out about my past, he'll be crushed. It will ruin his whole image of me."

I have heard these protests from various clients trying to hide their past. "Why dig it all up?" they ask. "Let that old affair stay buried in ancient history. Why not just leave that little demon alone?" I answer that it's not a little demon but an extremely important part of their personal story that says something about their habits and character.

But what if you haven't strayed since it happened? What if you've seen a pastor regularly to hold you accountable? Why put your spouse through the agony of a revelation that could ruin your relationship forever?

If that's your argument, I'd say you don't give your spouse much credit. Honesty and openness don't drive a spouse away—*dishonesty* does. When you hold something back, your spouse tries to guess what it is. If he or she is correct, then you must continually lie to cover your tracks. If incorrect, your spouse develops a false understanding of you and your predispositions.

Maybe you don't really want to be known for who you are. That's sad, isn't it? You'd rather keep your secret than experience one of life's greatest joys—to be loved and accepted in spite of known weaknesses.

While revealing your past will strengthen your marriage, it's not necessarily painless. Some spouses have difficulty adjusting to revelations that have been kept secret for years—the saint they thought they married turns out to be a mere mortal. To control the emotional damage of particularly shocking revelations, it may be helpful to express them to your spouse in the presence of a professional counselor. Some people may need some personal support to help them adjust to the reality of their spouse's past.

In cases I've witnessed, however, spouses tend to react more negatively to the long-term deception than to the concealed event. The thoughtless act might be accepted and forgiven, but the cover-up is often harder to understand. If you reveal it before your spouse discovers it, though, it's proof that you are taking honesty in your marriage seriously.

You may find the idea of revealing your past frightening, and that's understandable. But let me assure you that I've never seen a marriage destroyed by truth. When truth is revealed, there may be negative reactions and some shaky times, but ultimately the truth makes marriages stronger. On the other hand, hiding the truth destroys intimacy, romantic love, and marriages.

Current Honesty

In good marriages couples become so interdependent that sharing a daily schedule is essential to their coordination of activities. In weak marriages spouses are reluctant to reveal their schedules because they often engage in activities that they want to keep from each other. So they hide the details of their day, telling themselves, "What he doesn't know won't hurt him," or "She's happier not knowing everything."

But let's think back to Ted and Nicole for a moment. Ted's activities were innocent. He didn't do anything that would have been alarming to Nicole. By keeping them secret, however, Ted left Nicole's imagination to run wild. She even suspected that he might be having an affair. His failure to meet her basic need for honesty and openness prevented him from making Love Bank deposits. But her suspicions that he might be having an affair made huge Love Bank withdrawals. He could have made deposits and avoided withdrawals if he'd simply given her his daily schedule.

Make it easy for your spouse to find you in an emergency or to contact you during the day just to say hello. Keep your cell phones close by so that you can call each other 24/7.

Current Honesty

Reveal information about the events of your day. Provide your spouse with a calendar of your activities, with special emphasis on those that may affect him or her.

Current honesty protects your spouse from potentially damaging predispositions and inappropriate activities. When you know that you'll be telling your spouse what you've been up to, you're far less likely to have what I call a "secret second life." The easiest way to stay out of trouble is to shine a bright light on everything you do. Honesty and openness are that bright light.

Future Honesty

After I've made such a big issue of revealing past indiscretions, you can imagine how I feel about revealing future plans. They're *much* easier to discuss with your spouse, yet many couples make plans independently of each other. Why?

Some people believe that communicating future plans just gives a spouse the opportunity to quash them. They have their sights set on a certain goal and they don't want anything to stand in their way. But that's shortsighted thinking. If you keep your plans a secret, you may succeed in avoiding trouble in the present, but eventually the future will arrive and your plans will be revealed. And at that point your spouse will be hurt in two ways. First, because you didn't consider your spouse's feelings when you made your plans, and second, because you didn't tell your spouse about them. Love Bank withdrawals are certain to be made. So don't overlook this component of an honest and open relationship.

Future Honesty
Reveal your thoughts and plans regard-ing future activities and objectives.

I encourage spouses to make a date every Sunday afternoon at 3:30. The primary purpose of that date is to schedule fifteen hours of undivided attention for the coming week. If you don't schedule time for undivided attention, it won't happen, and you won't meet each other's most basic needs. But another purpose of your date is to review each other's entire schedule for the week. Each of you should know what the other is planning to do because almost everything you do will affect each other.

Encouraging Honesty

In this chapter, I have primarily focused attention on husbands and their unwillingness to be open and honest. But now I'd like to turn to wives. Do you do anything to discourage your husband in this area? More specifically, do your values encourage or discourage your husband to be open and honest with you? Do your reactions encourage or discourage your husband from revealing the truth, even when it's unpleasant? To see how you rate, answer these questions:

1. If the truth is terribly upsetting to you, do you want your spouse to be honest and open *only* at a time when you are emotionally prepared?

111

2. Do you keep some aspects of your life secret and do you encourage your spouse to respect *your* privacy in those areas?
3. Do you like to create a certain mystery between you and your spouse?
4. Are there subjects or situations about which you want to avoid radical honesty?
5. Do you ever make selfish demands when your spouse is open and honest with you?
6. Do you ever make disrespectful judgments when your spouse is open and honest with you?
7. Do you ever have angry outbursts when your spouse is open and honest with you?
8. Do you dwell on mistakes when your spouse is open and honest with you?

If you answer yes to any of the first four questions, you tend to compromise on the value of honesty and openness. Apparently you feel your marriage is better off with less information in certain situations. That little crack is all some husbands need to keep their distance emotionally. You see, there are always "reasons" to be less than radically honest. And as soon as you allow one to sneak in, it will invite all of its friends too. Before you know it, you'll have a marriage like Nicole and Ted's.

If you answered yes to questions 5, 6, 7, or 8, you are punishing honesty and openness. The way to help your spouse learn to be transparent is to minimize the negative consequences of his truthful revelations. If your spouse is faced with a fight whenever truth is revealed, he'll keep his thoughts to himself. But what if there are no demands, no judgments, no anger, no dwelling on mistakes? If you can eliminate these enemies of intimate conversation, you'll make it much easier for your spouse to be honest and open with you.

How Mutual Honesty Can Rescue a Marriage

What happens when a marriage so lacks honesty and openness that it leads to the ultimate dishonesty of an affair? Can coming clean with your spouse help or will it spell sure death for the relationship?

In a common scenario, I sit down to counsel with a husband who tells me, right up front, that he has been involved in a series of extramarital affairs. He has never told his wife about any of them yet he feels "terribly guilty" about all of them.

As therapy proceeds, I suggest that he confess all this to his wife. With some fear and trepidation he does so, and she responds with predictable reactions: anger, anxiety, and finally depression. In time, however, she somehow gets through the shock and pain. Then they can begin to build their marriage on mutual honesty, perhaps for the first time.

When a couple deal with trying to survive an affair, I train them to become thoroughly candid with each other. They must conceal nothing of what they think or feel. Only through total openness can an honest relationship emerge. If they compromise at any point, it will only undermine the rebuilding process.

You may wonder if it is always wise for the straying spouse to confess his or her sins to the other. In my experience, having the straying mate confess has never been the primary cause of a divorce. Some couples do go on to get a divorce because of the affair, but not because they have finally spoken honestly with each other. Instead, it's quite common for the betrayed spouse—husband or wife—to emerge from the initial shock of learning about the affair willing to examine and consider ways to resolve the marriage's problems. In chapter 13 of this book, How to Survive an Affair, I explain how to turn this willingness of the betrayed spouse to give the marriage a chance into complete marital recovery. In the end, trust is restored because the unfaithful spouse learns how to be honest and open.

A husband with a history of secrecy may insist that his confession of the affair by itself proves he has reformed. He may want his wife to begin to trust him again immediately. But here I disagree. You cannot turn on trust like a light switch. Rather, it takes numerous experiences of his honesty and openness to prove himself trustworthy to his wife.

As I mentioned earlier, I recommend strongly that the husband provide his wife with his daily schedule, which she can easily check for accuracy. If the schedule changes through the day, he should try his best to notify her immediately. She should be able to call some of the places he has listed on his schedule to verify his presence. Usually the couple can handle this process of verification in a way that avoids any embarrassment to either husband or wife.

The husband often resists having to provide his wife with this kind of information. He may complain about legalism, childish rule keeping, and he says, "All this checking will only prove she doesn't trust me after all." And that's just the point. She doesn't.

In response I simply comment that a well-organized person plans his schedule. Why should he be reluctant to share it with his wife? A wife should feel free to call her husband anytime during the day, even in relationships that exhibit no problem with trust. I provide that information to Joyce every day, and I've never had an affair. It's what people do who have great marriages.

With the procedure I've outlined, it may take years before trust is restored. Gradually, however, the wife finds, through repeated verification, that her husband is being honest with her.

The typical woman needs the ability to communicate with her husband any time of the day or night to sustain this feeling of openness and honesty. Most women will not abuse this privilege by calling their husband out of important meetings or otherwise interrupting him at work. However, the wife must know that she *can* call if she wants to and that, when she calls, her trust in her husband is confirmed.

Before we move on to the next chapter, I must make one other very important point regarding trust. While honesty and openness are essential in building trust, our behavior must also be trustworthy. Everything you decide to do must protect the feelings and interests of your spouse if you are to be trusted. If you tell your spouse everything you do each day yet do what you please with no regard for the effect it has on him or her, how do you expect your spouse to trust you? It's only when you are honest and open and also are making every decision with your spouse's interests in mind that you build a strong foundation for trust. I develop this important concept more fully in the opening chapters of *Love Busters*.

A woman *needs* to trust her husband. And her husband's openness and honesty with her goes a long way to enable her to do that. Whatever advantage a man may gain in being secretive, closed, or even dishonest, he gains at the expense of his wife's security and marital fulfillment. She must come to find him predictable; a blending of her mind with his should exist so that she can "read his mind." When a husband becomes that transparent, she is fulfilled—the two become one.

Questions for Him

1. What parts of my Policy of Radical Honesty are difficult for you—emotional honesty, historical honesty, current honesty, or future honesty? Why are they difficult?
2. Do you agree with the contention that there should be no privacy in your marriage—that is, neither one of you should keep facts regarding yourself from the other? Why or why not?
3. Does your wife encourage or discourage honesty and openness? Does she do this with her values and/or her reaction to your honesty?

Questions for Her

1. In your personal hierarchy of needs, how essential are your husband's honesty and openness? Do you agree that honesty and openness is one of your five basic needs in marriage? Why or why not?
2. Has your husband made it difficult for you to understand him? Has he kept his thoughts and feelings, personal history, current activities, or plans for the future from you? If so, how does this make you feel?
3. In what ways do you wish your husband were more open and honest with you? Do you wish for more emotional honesty, historical honesty, current honesty, and/or future honesty?

To Consider Together

1. Discuss your answers to the above questions. It will be a good test of how open and honest your marriage really is.
2. In the "Questionnaires" section of the Marriage Builders website (www.marriagebuilders.com), print two copies of the Personal History Questionnaire form, one for each of you. After you have com-

pleted the forms, read each other's answers and discuss them. Freely ask questions that are triggered by any of the answers you read.

3. If either of you needs help overcoming dishonesty, read together chapter 6, Dishonesty, in *Love Busters*. It will offer you a plan to help rid your marriage of this very destructive habit.

8

He Needs
a Good-Looking Wife—
Physical Attractiveness

At twenty-six and 190 pounds, Brittany seldom had dates—four in the last two years to be exact and no calls back after the first one. Her prospects for marriage seemed bleak, to say the least. Even though she had a charming personality and many interests, few men wanted to date her.

One day Brittany decided she had to make a change. She wanted to marry and she was tired of her job. *If I had someone to take care of me,* she thought, *I could quit the job and do something I'd enjoy. I'd like that.* As her first tactic in achieving that goal, Brittany enrolled in an exercise program, went on a diet, and lost sixty pounds. Next she bought some new clothes that nicely accentuated her slender figure. A new hairdo and appropriate makeup completed the transformation.

With sixty pounds gone and the other improvements, Brittany was a real knockout. Now she had dates right and left but she had not forgotten her goal—a husband. About eight months later, when Josh proposed, she said yes. She had achieved her goal with great speed.

When I counseled Brittany and Josh about five years later, I started by talking with them separately. Josh told me, "The first thing she did after we were married was quit her job. Then she stayed home, eating like mad all day. She blew up like a balloon—she's gained about a hundred pounds since we've been married."

"Have you said anything about her weight?" I asked.

"Yes, many times. In fact it's a sore point between us. But she just says, 'I want you to love me for who I am. If you'd love me and accept me unconditionally, then I could easily lose the weight.' But the less I say, the more weight she gains," Josh continued. "I am finding myself more attracted to other women. I can't handle this, and something has to happen."

As we continued to talk, I could see that Josh faced a real dilemma. Reared in a conservative church, he had held strong convictions about being faithful, but he found himself married to a wife whose figure repulsed him. He had almost no interest in making love with her anymore. When he married her, he had looked forward to a happy future with a wife who was very physically attractive to him. But now life with Brittany seemed like a prison sentence. He believed his only hope for a romantic relationship was in having an affair. And his convictions were weakening.

Next I talked to Brittany to get her side. She confessed to me that she had launched a self-improvement program to get dates and a husband, and also admitted that she had never told Josh that she had once weighed so much. When she married Josh, she thought he would love her regardless of her weight and that she could go back to being fat and happy. So when he told her he was tempted to be in another relationship, she felt terribly hurt. She had thought that once Josh got to know and love her, her weight would no longer matter to him. But she was wrong.

Granted, some men do not care about physical appearance. Their wives can be overweight or underweight; it makes no difference. They have other emotional needs that are far more important than the need for physical attractiveness. But Brittany had not married one of these men. In fact she had married a man for whom physical appearance was near the very top of his list. He needed an attractive wife.

Some women also have a need for an attractive husband. Many wives I've counseled have given their husband the ultimate threat—either lose weight or our marriage is over. One woman I counseled would not live with her husband until he lost fifty pounds.

Brittany listened intently as I explained that a marriage commitment means meeting the basic needs of your spouse. She wanted Josh to earn a good living, be affectionate to her, and talk with her often, which he had done since they had been married. But she wasn't holding up her end of the bargain.

"What do you mean, not holding up my end?" she snapped. "I cook good meals. I keep the house clean. I'm affectionate . . ."

"All that is good, but you're missing something," I explained. "Your physical attractiveness is *very* important to your husband. This isn't some quirk or whim. It's something he needs *very* badly. The beautiful woman he married hides under all that excess weight. By taking care of your body, you take care of your husband."

Brittany didn't quite hear me at first. She persisted in arguing, "Josh should love me as I am!"

"We all want to be loved for who we are and not for what we do," I said. "But you didn't decide to marry your husband for who he is, but rather for what he did. If he had not met any of your basic emotional needs when you dated him, you would not have even considered him as a life partner. And if after you were married, he stopped meeting those needs, your feelings for him would have changed considerably. Your love would have faded away, and just like Josh, you would have felt trapped."

Many men think that the emotional needs of women, such as affection and intimate conversation, are trivial needs. Many women think that the emotional needs of men are trivial. But they are not trivial to those who have them. Even though Brittany knew she had to have a slim figure to attract a husband, she thought that physical attractiveness was trivial because she didn't have that need. So she concluded that Josh's shallow sense of values was the culprit. If he would grow up and be more mature, he would look beyond her appearance and she could gain as much weight as she wanted.

Why All the Fuss about Looking Good?

People often challenge me when I list physical attractiveness as one of the basic emotional needs of most men. In fact, some have written me saying that when they came to this chapter, they lost all confidence in my judgment. Shouldn't we be looking beyond the surface and into more meaningful human characteristics, such as honesty, trust, and caring? Besides, what if a woman simply can't look attractive because of her heredity? Does that mean she's destined to be unloved?

As I mentioned earlier, not all men have a basic need for physical attractiveness. They marry women who meet other basic needs. But in Josh's case, he chose Brittany because she met this need so effectively while they were dating. And Brittany worked hard to look attractive right up to the day of their wedding. If she had wanted to marry a man who would accept a heavier woman, she should not have lost the weight prior to dating.

Besides gaining weight after her wedding, Brittany also quit her job. But Josh never complained about that change, because he didn't have a need that I'll introduce in the next chapter—the need for financial support. He was happy to support her financially, as long as she met his basic emotional needs.

What if Josh had left his job, expecting Brittany to support him? Would she have accepted him the way he was? This argument, that Josh should have the right to leave his job if she has the right to gain weight, finally convinced Brittany. She realized that if he decided to stay at home and let her support him, she wouldn't be accepting him so unconditionally. The only reason she felt unconditional love for him was that he was already meeting her basic emotional needs—an essential condition for her continuing love for him.

So she enrolled in an exercise program, went on a diet, and lost forty pounds in three months. Once Josh saw she meant business, he joined her in the exercise program. A year later she had lost the weight she'd gained since their wedding.

Brittany's program of self-improvement was not only a gesture of care for Josh. It was also a very effective way to care for herself. Once she got down to a desirable weight, Josh liked the result, and she did too. It greatly improved her health and feeling of self-esteem.

Beauty, of course, is in the eye of the beholder, and I am not encouraging a wife to try to look like a beauty queen. I simply mean that she should try to look the way her husband likes her to look. She should resemble the woman he married.

Does that mean a woman must stay eternally young? Of course not, but getting old is not an excuse for gaining weight and dressing poorly. This is exactly what Brittany had done, and it made Josh feel cheated.

Josh and Brittany's story ended happily, but many do not. I have counseled other wives (and husbands) who have refused to improve their physical appearance. In doing so, they miss an opportunity to provide essential care to their mate that would make huge Love Bank deposits. They also greatly increase the risk of their spouse having an affair.

When She Looks Good, He Feels Good

A man with a need for an attractive spouse feels good whenever he looks at his attractive wife. In fact that's what emotional needs are all about. When one of his emotional needs is met, he feels fulfilled; and when it's not met, he feels frustrated. It may sound immature or superficial to some, but I've found that most men have a need for physical attractiveness. They appreciate a good-looking wife.

Women want their husband to look decent and they might admit that attractive men get their attention, but I've found that most women do not rank physical attraction among their top five emotional needs. They are far more likely to fall in love with men who meet other basic emotional needs, such as affection, intimate conversation, honesty and openness, financial support, and family commitment.

I remember an overweight, balding man who was twenty years older than his very pretty wife. Nonetheless, she was crazy about him and they shared a very active sex life. What did she see in him? That's just the point. Instead of looking *at* him, she looked *within* him and found a warm and sensitive man, kind and generous, who loved her as deeply as she loved him. To her he was "rather nice looking."

Was she more mature than her husband, who was admittedly attracted by her appearance? No. She simply had different emotional needs. For her, physical attractiveness did not do as much for her as it did for him. She put effort into making herself look good because she knew it would make him happy. In return, he put effort into meeting her needs for affection, intimate conversation, and financial support.

Any woman can enhance her attractiveness to her husband. There are plenty of books, videos, diet programs, and other products designed to help women (and men) shape up, dress with style, color their hair properly, and so forth. When I counsel wives who want to improve their physical appearance, I focus attention on five major areas that are particularly important in staying or becoming attractive. Let's give them a quick survey.

The "Secret" to Weight Control

Every year several new books appear offering the latest "foolproof" diet or weight-control plan. Here's mine, Harley's Second Corollary:

> *Balance your intake of calories with the proper amount of exercise.*

I'm sorry I can't sound more sensational, effortless, or intriguing, but there is no "secret" to weight and figure control. It takes discipline, and that's been known for centuries.

I counsel many women who just don't believe me. They keep hoping for some revolutionary new gimmick that will solve their weight problem with little or no effort, or they crash diet and soon gain it all back. Then they crash again and again. Sooner or later they give up, heavier than ever.

The truth is that weight-control programs work only when they are a way of life, based on the facts of life. All human bodies, including female ones, are machines that burn fuel. When the body takes in too much fuel and doesn't burn it off, it stores the fuel in the form of fat. So if you want to avoid getting fat, you must burn all the fuel your body takes in. To lose weight, you must burn even more fuel.

Fuel, of course, is what you eat, and you burn it with exercise. You burn some of it by just sitting around, but it burns much faster with exercise. If you exercise often, you can afford to eat more because you're burning more fuel. From my perspective, however, it's much easier to eat less than it is to exercise more.

A popular approach to dieting is to consume four three-hundred-calorie meals a day, spaced four hours apart. Healthy frozen three-hundred-calorie meals that can be prepared in a microwave oven are readily available in grocery stores. When a woman limits her food intake to these four meals a day, she usually loses about two pounds a week if she eats nothing else. Most men can eat five of these meals a day with the same results.

Yes, I know, you think you are addicted to food. But so is everybody—we all die of hunger without it. Hunger is a normal reaction to weight loss because our bodies are programmed to prevent weight loss. But that doesn't mean you can't eat less—it simply means you will be somewhat hungry while you're doing it. But by eating small meals four hours apart, you will minimize your hunger.

Keep your intake of sugar and fat to a minimum. If you are tempted to binge on something with lots of calories (ice cream or potato chips, for example), don't even buy it. That may be the only way to avoid being out of control. Your children and your husband may complain, but they'll be as healthy as you.

Aerobic exercise will help you lose even more of the extra pounds, while keeping your heart and lungs healthy. All it takes is enough exercise to increase your heart rate 60–70 percent of its maximum for about 30 minutes every other day. (To find your maximum heart rate, subtract your age from 220; then to find your best aerobic heart rate for your age, multiply your maximum heart rate by .70.)

Joyce and I share the same diet program, and we also exercise with each other whenever possible. We encourage each other in weight control. Both of us come from families where there has been a tendency to gain weight in later years, and we have made an agreement with each other to avoid that outcome.

If you have agreed to lose weight and keep it off, you must create a new lifestyle around diet and exercise, and your spouse should be a part of it. It may mean that he will avoid foods that are not on your diet and join you in an exercise program. When both of you are committed to this new lifestyle, the chances that it will succeed are greatly increased.

The Use of Makeup

Rose came into my office looking more like a clown than a well–made-up woman. Although she might have had some attractive features, they lay buried beneath a mass of colors vying for attention. In her effort to make herself attractive, something had gone wrong. She hadn't used the makeup to her advantage.

Cosmetics have been around since ancient Egyptian times, and with our modern multibillion-dollar cosmetic industry no woman has the excuse that help is not available. Most women who use no makeup or use it inappropriately simply lack the initiative to get the help they need.

Some women have never learned to apply makeup to their best advantage. As in Rose's case, I sometimes step in where angels fear to tread and suggest that she might seek professional advice. Some cosmetic studios or large department stores provide free consultations. Of course much depends on the knowledge of the person who gives the consultation, but many can give good advice. Women's magazines also publish articles that will help achieve the same goal. I've found that eye makeup along with eyebrow shaping tend to be the most important.

I have seen many women make dramatic improvements in their appearance just by applying makeup more effectively. Almost always when single women make these changes, single men pay more attention and ask them out on dates. The husbands of women who make an effort to improve their use of makeup appreciate and encourage the change if their wife has done it for them. While your objective is to meet his need for physical attractiveness, you should also like the change as well. Don't use cosmetics in a way that makes you feel uncomfortable.

A Hairstyle He Likes

Most women are particularly sensitive to how their hair looks. Yearly they spend billions on dyes, rinses, shampoos, perms, sets, and cuts. My questions are, why and for whom?

If a wife spends all that time and money to please her husband and to achieve something she likes, well and good. But if she lets some hairdresser talk her into something she knows her husband won't like, she has begun to work against herself—and her marriage.

A certain hair color manufacturer excuses the higher price of their product by telling the woman, "You're worth it." More to the point, your husband is worth it. If he doesn't like a certain hairstyle and color, abandon it. In fact, consult with him ahead of time and get his opinion before ever getting a different style or color. After all, the whole idea is to be attractive to him.

Or is it? Some women object to this idea. They insist on the right to please themselves or they argue that having to please their husband in such a way seems unfair and even degrading.

I don't encourage women to accept meekly a hairstyle that makes them miserable. Certainly they need to enjoy their own looks and feel attractive. If a husband likes something his wife can't tolerate, negotiation is in order. Among the many hairstyles available, I'm certain they can find one on which they can agree.

Hairstyles, like everything else, can create deposits or withdrawals in a husband's Love Bank. If a wife understands her husband's need for physical attractiveness, she will work with him to achieve that goal. In my experience, chances are great that she will find that her husband has fairly good taste.

The Importance of the Right Clothes

The old adage tells us, "Clothes make the man," but in our society, clothes showcase the woman. That showcase can enhance and flatter—or do something far less than that. As with cosmetics and hairstyle, the same principle applies: dress to be attractive to your husband and comfortable with your own look.

Fashions come and go, and in certain years clothing styles range from silly to disastrous. Despite the insistence of some clothes designers to be eternally creative, one rule still seems to prevail: when women's clothing becomes unappealing to most men, it does not stay popular very long.

A woman should pay as much, if not more, attention to her choice of nightgown or pajamas as she does to what she wears in public. When she dresses for bed, she dresses strictly for her husband. Wearing old and bedraggled nightclothes, curlers, and goop on her face will *not* make Love Bank deposits. Wearing a worn-out nightgown to bed because "nobody will see it" misses an important point. One very special and important person does see it, so why not wear something attractive? Your husband will certainly appreciate it.

Personal Hygiene

To be honest, I've hardly ever counseled a woman who needed help with her personal hygiene but I've helped many men with this problem. Since the need for an attractive spouse is sometimes a wife's need, hygiene is a subject that should be addressed in this chapter.

Kent was a very successful farmer; he was worth millions. When he asked Jessica to marry him, all she could think about was his millions. He was a decent man but, having been single for the better part of his adult life, had paid little attention to his appearance. Jessica thought she could overlook his outward appearance and love him for his inner qualities—and his money. After they were married, however, she found his appearance turned her off completely.

When they came for their first appointment, Kent complained that Jessica refused to make love to him. She came up with every excuse, and he finally thought a counselor might help.

"I just can't have sex with him," she explained. "When I married him, I thought he would be more appealing to me, but it's getting worse. He'll probably divorce me, but I just can't do it."

When Kent came into the office, his body odor just about knocked me over! He had been chewing tobacco and his teeth were caked with residue. His hair was a mess, and his clothes looked like he'd slept in them. I had counseled many men who had trouble keeping themselves clean, but Kent was beyond anything I could have imagined.

"She doesn't like sex," was his explanation for their problem.

I had a different theory. "I think I can help you," I replied, "but you'll have to do everything I recommend. Within a few weeks I think your problem will be solved."

I gave him this assignment:

1. Take a shower every morning and evening.
2. With Jessica's help, buy a new wardrobe of clothes. Let Jessica pick out clothes for you to wear each day. Never wear anything you've worn the day before unless it has been washed.
3. Go to a dentist and have your teeth cleaned. Never chew tobacco in Jessica's presence and brush your teeth before being with her.
4. Comb your hair and shave every morning before breakfast.

Fulfilling this assignment was quite a commitment for Kent. He was used to going weeks without a shower. He wore the same pants and shirt day after day and he hadn't been to a dentist since he was a teenager. But he agreed to it, believing me when I said it would help his sexual relationship with Jessica.

Then I gave Jessica her assignment. Shop with Kent for clothes, pick out something for him to wear every day, and see to it that the clothes are clean. I also asked her if she would be willing to make love to him every day for just one week after he followed through on his assignment.

A deal was struck and Kent was off to the dentist and clothing store. He kept his part of the bargain, and Jessica kept hers. After he had clean teeth, clean clothes, and a clean body, Jessica made love to him once a day for a week.

At their next appointment, I could hardly recognize Kent. What a transformation! And they were holding hands in the waiting room. All on their own, without my counsel, they had made a long-term agreement. She would make love to him if he would keep himself clean. Their sexual problems were over.

I'm sure they didn't make love every day from then on, but they were both satisfied with their new sexual compatibility. Kent had learned a very important lesson about Jessica. His physical appearance, especially his smell, was important to her sexually. At first, she wanted to believe that outward appearances were not important, that she should love him in spite of his appearance, but the changes he made in his personal hygiene proved that her need for an attractive spouse was greater than she had been willing to admit.

The hygiene problems of most men are not as extreme as Kent's, but lesser problems can still have a devastating effect on wives, especially while making love. A woman wants to be physically close to the man she loves, especially if he looks and smells good.

The Value of Making the Most of What You Have

If you are still unconvinced that physical attractiveness is a worthy objective, consider what it means to be physically attractive. It simply means that your appearance makes someone feel good. You meet an emotional need by the way you look. People can be attractive in many ways. Those with attractive personalities may also meet an emotional need, but they usually deposit love units with the quality of their conversation or affection, rather than their appearance. In fact, whenever someone meets any of our emotional needs, we consider that person attractive. If physical attractiveness meets an emotional need of your spouse, why ignore it? Why not deposit love units whenever you have a chance?

For some, like Brittany at the beginning of this chapter, the prospect of becoming physically attractive seems completely out of reach. These women have fallen for the lie that some women are born attractive while others are not. But they can discover the truth of Harley's Third Corollary:

Attractiveness is what you do with what you have.

Every woman would benefit from evaluating each aspect of the image she projects—her posture, hairstyle, clothing, gestures, makeup, weight, and so forth. She should ask her husband for his honest appraisal and, if possible, consult professionals or trustworthy friends. Then she should decide where change is needed and set realistic goals for making those changes. For some, the changes might be completed in a week, while for others, it could take years. But in the end, the makeover would have such significance that it would be life changing—for the better.

Lydia, a client who suffered from depression, demonstrated dramatically how a woman can profit from an improved appearance. This exceptionally bright and charming woman wanted dates with men who were truly on a par with her, but she had not given her appearance the attention it needed. I reminded her how important appearance is to most men. Granted, it was not one of her emotional needs—she could not have cared less how the men she dated looked. But it was likely that the man of her dreams would have a need for a wife who was physically attractive, and if she wanted to attract him, she would have to meet this need.

Her metamorphosis took six months to accomplish. At the end of that time, Lydia was a stunningly attractive woman. Men she already knew and liked started dating her. Her depression disappeared entirely, and she no longer needed my services.

When I saw Lydia for the last time, I reminded her not to make the same mistake that Brittany had made—shaping up to attract a man and then letting herself go after marriage. Lydia knew that the changes she had made to attract a husband would have to be permanent because the emotional need she could meet by being attractive would continue to be there after marriage.

If you know how to make your spouse feel good, doesn't it make sense to go ahead and do it—whenever you can? Often a wife's attractiveness is a vital ingredient to the success of her marriage, and any woman who ignores this notion, for whatever reasons, risks disaster. This is true for some men as well. The changes in appearance I've witnessed in my clients have not only met spouses' needs but have also made my clients feel much better about themselves. The changes have made them more successful in business and have improved their health. It's one of those efforts that pays dividends in ways that go far beyond the marriage itself.

When a woman sees her husband's response to her improved appearance, she knows that she's made the right decision because it has met one of his basic needs. Her account in his Love Bank will get a substantial deposit every time he sees her.

Questions for Her

1. Do you take your husband's need for you to be attractive seriously? If not, why not?
2. Does your husband really like the way you look most of the time? Do you?
3. How much care do you take in the way you look? How is your figure? Do you use cosmetics to good advantage? Do you change your hairstyle from time to time to please your husband by giving him a little variety in the way you look?

Questions for Him

1. Are you willing to admit that physical attractiveness is one of your most basic needs in your marriage? If not, why not?

2. Has your wife's appearance become less attractive since your wedding? Do you really like the way she looks or do you just say you do?

3. If your wife told you she was willing to change anything she could about her physical appearance, what would you ask her to change? Why?

To Consider Together

1. Sit down with your collection of photographs—especially those from the days when you were dating and from your wedding day. Compare the way you looked then with the way you look today. Do you need to make some changes? How?

2. Share your answers to the above questions with each other. Be respectful but honest.

3. How can you help your spouse become more physically attractive to you?

9

She Needs Enough Money to Live Comfortably— Financial Support

Taylor had been raised in an upper-middle-class American home. She attended the state university where she majored in art, history—and Jon. They married while still in school.

Jon finished his undergraduate work and also earned a master's degree in fine arts. But once he was out of school, he could find no work that utilized his training. He tried to move into the world of commercial art, but the competition was fierce. Two years after graduation, he had still not found full-time work. He kept very busy with his painting and drawing, but his income was poor and unpredictable. During the first six years of their marriage, his jobs or assignments never lasted longer than six months.

Consequently, Taylor found herself working full-time as a receptionist to help make ends meet. She wanted to have children, but their finances prevented it. They lived in a modest apartment. Little money was available for extras, and they could afford only one inexpensive car.

Taylor knew several young executives at work who had started to climb the ladder of success. They all looked terrific to Taylor, dressed handsomely in thousand-dollar suits. Some were already earning incomes several times higher than Jon's would ever be.

Alan was one of those executives and he was attracted to Taylor. On several occasions she had helped him make sales by her skillful handling of customers on the telephone and in the lobby. That had motivated him to work more closely with her and from time to time he would stop by her desk just to talk. The more he got to know her, the more he liked her.

During those conversations, Alan often heard Taylor say things like, "I feel so bad for Jon. He's so good at what he does, but it's hard for an artist to find a steady job." One day she broke down and started crying.

"Taylor!" His voice conveyed more compassion than alarm.

"I don't think Jon will ever earn much," she sobbed. "We'll never have anything."

"It's probably none of my business, but Jon has a good thing going," Alan suggested. "He can spend all day enjoying art while you're here supporting him. If he hadn't married you, he'd be working like the rest of us. I don't think he's being fair to you."

That started Taylor thinking. *Jon is using me!* she thought. *He's doing what he enjoys at my expense. If he cared about me, he'd give up his artwork for a profession that could support us.* She became increasingly resentful about how trapped she was.

As time went by, Taylor and Alan became good friends. They began to talk sales, first at her desk at odd moments, then at coffee breaks, and finally at lunch almost every day. He reminded Taylor of her father who was also a businessman—ambitious and prosperous. The more she came to know Alan, the more she felt it had been a mistake to marry Jon.

By predictable stages, the friendship grew into an affair. The weekend Jon had gone out of town to interview for a part-time teaching position, Alan invited Taylor to join him on his boat. That was the first of many times they made love.

The job didn't come through, but it started Taylor thinking that someday she might be forced to move away from Alan so Jon could take a job somewhere else. Or worse yet, Jon might discover her affair. To avoid those and other unpleasant prospects, she filed for divorce. A year later she married Alan.

Do Women Marry Men for Their Money?

Humorous anecdotes abound about women who marry men for their money, but my counseling experience has taught me not to treat this tendency as a joke. In truth a woman *does* marry a man for his money—she wants him to earn at least enough to support *himself.*

I can recall talking to a woman who had a problem very similar to Taylor's. Her marriage was intensely unhappy due to her husband's low income, but she insisted she would never "stoop to divorce" to resolve the problem.

"Don is loyal and affectionate. I'd never be so selfish and uncaring as to leave him just because he doesn't make enough money."

"Oh," I replied, "do you always feel that way?"

"Of course I do! Leaving a man who doesn't make enough money is a lowdown, selfish thing to do." Olivia seemed to know her mind and convinced me that she would stick it out. Two weeks later she missed her appointment with me because she had filed for divorce and felt too ashamed to tell me about it. After the divorce was finalized, she married a man who earned considerably more money than her former husband.

Why did Olivia make such loud protests against "stooping to divorce" when in the end she did not really have that strong a commitment to marriage? Actually she didn't exhibit very unusual behavior. I counsel many people who become what I call "verbally rigid" just before they crack. I believe Olivia's inconsistent actions resulted from a struggle deep within her between her values and her need for financial support. The incredibly powerful need to have enough money won over all her commitment and good intentions.

For the past fifty years, we've witnessed a revolution in the workforce. When I started my career as a psychologist, men dominated the field. My class of twenty-five Ph.D. candidates included only two women. Today women dominate psychology. But the revolution has not affected only my profession. Overall, women now outnumber men in most careers; they are in the working majority.

So you might think that the cultural shift toward women in the workplace would change a woman's need for financial support. Apparently, that's not been the case.

As a test of whether women still marry for money, I will sometimes ask an audience of young couples a question. "If just before your marriage, your spouse had announced that you should not expect him or her to earn an income, would you have tied the knot? Raise your hand if you would have gone through with the wedding." While almost all of the men have their hands raised, hardly a single woman's hand joins them. That's because most women still expect their husband to earn a living. They still have an emotional need for financial support.

Resentment for *Having* to Work

Most wives expect their husband not only to work but to earn enough to support their family. Time after time married women have told me they resent *having* to work. The women I talk to usually want a *choice* between following a career and being a homemaker—or possibly they want a combination of the two. Often they want to be homemakers in their younger years, while their children are small. Later, when the children have grown, they want to develop careers outside the home.

However, hard reality for many women today dictates that they must work to help make ends meet, even when their children are small. Their husbands simply can't handle the basic monthly bills on their own.

Please understand I'm not against women who want careers and I don't oppose women who choose a career early in life. My daughter earned a Ph.D. degree and is a licensed psychologist. She raised her two daughters while employed. I am proud of her achievement, and she is happy with her dual role as homemaker and psychologist. And so is her husband.

I wish, rather, to stress the principle that many women need to have the *choice* of whether or not to work once they have children. If they *do* choose a career, the money they earn should not have to be spent on basic support of the family. To put it all very simply, many families need to learn how to live on what a husband can earn in a normal workweek.

If a couple can "bite the bullet" and lower an unrealistic standard of living, that action frees the husband to set realistic economic objectives regarding the family's basic financial needs. But as long as the wife keeps working so that together they can finance the big house, big cars, and everyone's credit card habit, where is the incentive to cut back?

I realize what I say will not be popular with many couples. Many will simply write me off as unrealistic. Don't I know that today a couple simply cannot live on one salary? No, I really don't know that, as I will explain later in this chapter. In fact I know that a family *can* live on one salary and I will show you how it can be done. I simply want to emphasize that there are many women whose need for financial support is deep and should be treated seriously. Most men don't have this need. Rarely does a husband feel good when his wife supports him financially. If his salary pays the bills, he will probably feel quite content if she earns little or nothing. By contrast, I have met very few women who sincerely feel content with a husband who earns little or nothing.

Some well-intentioned people, in the guise of advocating women's rights, encourage all women to develop a career, because they see employment as a right and privilege. However, they fail to consider that a woman also has a right and privilege to be a homemaker and full-time mother. Sometimes those who argue that women should choose a career fail to understand their needs as mothers. I believe that women should have the choice of homemaking or career. When that choice is made for them by their husband, women's rights advocates, or anyone else, it deprives many of them of marital fulfillment.

The Necessary Good—a Budget

Every family must come to grips with what it can afford. Some couples look on budgets as a "necessary evil." I like to call a budget a "necessary good" and I recommend it to almost every couple I counsel. I have yet to meet a couple who at times didn't want to buy more than they could afford.

A budget helps you discover what a certain quality of life really costs. To more fully understand the quality of life you can afford, I recommend three budgets: one to describe what you *need*, one to describe what you *want*, and one to describe what you can *afford*.

The *needs budget* should include the monthly cost of meeting the necessities of your life, items you would be uncomfortable without.

The *wants budget* includes the cost of meeting all your needs and wants—things that bring special pleasure to your life. It should be realistic, however. No mansions or chauffeur-driven limos if these lie totally out of your range.

The *affordable budget* begins with your income and should first include the cost of the needs budget. If there's money left over when the cost of meeting all your needs is covered, your most important wants are then included in this budget until your expenses match your income.

To put these budgets in the context of need for financial support, I recommend that only the husband's income be used in the needs budget. In other words, if his income is sufficient to meet all the needs of the family, by definition he has met his wife's need for financial support. Without these budgets, his success in meeting this need may not be obvious to her.

Both the husband's and wife's incomes are included in the wants budget. If her income when added to his covers all of their needs and wants, they must go no further. But if the cost of their needs and wants outstrip their joint income, the affordable budget strips away their lowest priority wants, leaving them with needs covered by his income and wants they can afford covered by her income. These three budgets make it clear that the wife's income is helping the family improve its quality of life, providing for wants that are beyond their basic needs.

Some women want to work for the challenges of a career; for others it's to escape from the children. But regardless of the reason, if her husband's income supports the family's basic needs, she's not working to support herself or her family. She may decide that she'll have a higher quality of life by *not* working as much. She may not have as much money but she has more time with her family.

I've been amazed by the number of women who feel much better toward their husband when they realize that his income actually pays for her needs and those of the children. The Financial Support Inventory, appendix D, will help you create a needs budget, wants budget, and affordable budget.

Can He Earn More?

But what happens when a husband's income is not sufficient to pay for the needs budget expenses? Lowering their standard of living will be a very distasteful option for many women. Resentful as they might be about working, they may prefer that to lowering their basic quality of life.

I've met countless couples caught in this trap. He works as hard as he can, coming home tired every night, but his paycheck just won't go far enough. His wife faces the impossible choice of being unhappy while working to make up the difference or being unhappy while putting up with what seems to her an intolerably poor quality of life. His account in her Love Bank is being drained. *How much longer can I put up with it?* she wonders.

I sympathize with the man trapped in this situation. He does the best he can yet cannot meet his wife's emotional need for financial support. Isn't there an answer to this kind of impasse? Somehow he must increase his income without sacrificing time with his family. He can try to obtain a raise in pay or a job that pays more, or he may need to go to the trouble of a career change. The following story illustrates how one couple solved this problem.

When Sean and Mindy came to me for counseling, Sean's career had reached a plateau. He had advanced about as far as he could with the company where he worked. I saw Mindy first, and she broke into tears. "I suppose I shouldn't feel this way but I am losing respect for Sean. He can't earn enough to pay our bills and now he wants me to go back to work to make up the difference. With the children so young, I just don't want to do that."

"What about cutting back on expenses?" I asked.

"As far as I'm concerned we're at the bare minimum now. I suppose we couldn't afford a bigger house, but now we're in it. And we could never get along without a second car. We just live too far out for me to be home alone without some kind of transportation."

I could see that talking to Mindy about lowering her quality of life was pointless, so I pulled out the only other card in my hand. "Perhaps Sean could earn quite a bit more if he finished his education—I believe you said he had two years left. Would you be willing to go to work to help him?"

"Well, I suppose I could—just so it wouldn't be forever," Mindy replied. "I'll talk to Sean and see what he thinks."

Within a few weeks Sean and Mindy had it worked out. She had found a full-time job, and his company had allowed him to take a part-time position so he could attend college and finish his degree.

Their new plan saved their marriage. Mindy was pleased to see Sean trying to improve his income-producing potential and she did not mind the sacrifice, because she knew it wouldn't be permanent. Ironically enough, Mindy loved her job so much that she continued working even after Sean had completed school and began earning enough to support the family. In the end she gained respect for her husband *and* a valued career for herself.

If a husband's income is truly insufficient, he should try to improve his job skills. While he is training for this new job, the family may temporarily lower its standard of living, his wife may go to work, or perhaps both adjustments will be made. I have found that most women are willing to lower their quality of life and go to work to help support the family if it is a *temporary* solution to a financial crisis. This temporary sacrifice can actually prove to be a powerful builder of rapport and affection in the marriage. When a husband and wife work together toward a common goal, their interests are much more likely to overlap, and their conversations will become more interesting to each other. In short, they become a winning team; and players on a winning team usually like and respect one another.

How to Live on One Thousand Dollars per Month

Having counseled so many couples like Sean and Mindy, I've become aware of how little it costs to be happy. As a short-term measure, while education is being completed, couples learn to cut their costs to the bone. Once the changes are made, they're often amazed at how satisfied they are living on a shoestring.

When I first met Sarah and Jim, they had set themselves adrift and seemed headed for the financial rocks. Both worked full-time, but things they bought with their dual income gave them little pleasure. They became addicted to drugs and alcohol, abandoned their moral values, and seemed destined to self-destruct.

When they came to see me, I convinced them they both needed a new direction in life and that a college education was a good place to find that direction. They had only one problem—they were accustomed to living on their combined incomes of nine thousand dollars a month and they could never earn that much and attend school too.

I suggested a radical solution. "Have you ever lived on one thousand dollars a month?" I asked.

They looked at each other and started to laugh. "No one *can* live on one thousand dollars a month," Jim responded.

"Oh, on the contrary, most people in the world live on less than half that much. You might find it interesting to experiment and see how the rest of the world does it."

The two of them left my office that day still chuckling and shaking their heads, but I had planted the seed. It took them several weeks to make the decision, and I am certain they thought the experiment would become something like joining VISTA or the Peace Corps. Nonetheless, we worked out the following monthly budget:

Housing and utilities	$ 400
Groceries	$ 200
Clothes	$ 100
Miscellaneous and emergencies	$ 300
Total	$1,000

They rented a single room with an area for cooking, near the university they attended. Because they had sold their cars, they rode the bus or biked to school and work. They bought nourishing but inexpensive food. All their clothing purchases were at thrift shops. They already had acquired their furniture. The money from the sale of their cars and unneeded possessions went into savings.

Each of them worked only fifteen hours a week to earn the thousand dollars they needed. They actually earned more once in a while, but agreed not to spend more. Now they could not afford drugs or alcohol and had to overcome their habits. They even had to give up smoking. Funding for their education came almost completely from grants. When they completed their education, they still had money in their savings account.

I witnessed the change in their lives. Because the credits in their Love Banks had risen, they were undeniably happy. Their marriage, about to end in divorce when I first saw them, now flourished. This change took place *while* they lived on a thousand dollars a month.

It's possible to live on much less than we do. I am not trying to convince you that you should live on a thousand dollars a month. Surely families with children would face serious challenges. But almost any family *can* live comfortably on less than they presently spend. I simply want you to consider the idea that many people think they need things they may not really need. Sometimes they become their own worst enemies. They sacrifice the fulfillment of their marital need for financial support by creating a standard of living they cannot afford. Many men work themselves to an early grave providing what their families can do without. Sometimes we may measure the cost of high living standards in the loss of life's most valuable treasures.

Together you may prove the truth of Harley's Fourth Corollary:

> *When it comes to money and marriage,*
> *less may be more.*

Questions for Him

1. When you first married, did you think your wife would expect you to support her financially? Did you expect her to work?
2. Do you think your wife is satisfied with the money you can presently earn working a normal workweek?
3. Have you recently considered retraining so that you could qualify for a job that pays more? Would cutting household expenses accomplish the same objective?

Questions for Her

1. Have you thought much about your husband's income and how it affects your standard of living? If so, how do you feel about it?
2. Would you feel comfortable sharing with him any negative feelings you may have about his level of income? Have you shared these feelings in the past?

3. Are you willing to reduce your standard of living so your husband's income will support you? Do you want to be able to choose between a career and raising a family full-time?

To Consider Together

1. What is your current standard of living? Do you both feel happy with it? Do you really have enough money to meet it?
2. Use the form Financial Support Inventory, appendix D, to create a needs budget, a wants budget, and an affordable budget.
3. Should you make some changes? Would retraining help? Would reducing your standard of living help? Decide together how to implement needed changes.

He Needs
Peace and Quiet—
Domestic Support

10

Phil was a prosperous young bachelor. His job paid well. Because he had made a substantial down payment, his car payments were low. His apartment was pleasant, nicely furnished, and well situated. He had dated a number of women before he met Charlene, but she turned out to be different—special. They became best friends, and after about eight months of dating, he asked her to marry him.

The wedding took place in October. At first, they lived in his apartment, but that was just to give them time to finish accumulating the money to put down on a house. Because Charlene had a good job too, they had no trouble pooling their resources to become homeowners.

The next summer they found the place they wanted and they moved by September. Phil relished many of the responsibilities of owning a home—caring for the yard, making repairs, installing new fixtures, and so forth.

Everything went well until their first child arrived. Then Charlene decided to cut back to part-time work. That cut their income at a time when their expenses escalated. Phil took a second job to compensate for the loss of

Charlene's income. He found himself working twelve-hour days, first as manager of his department, then as a part-time bookkeeper for another company.

At the end of five years, Phil and Charlene had three children. Phil still worked two jobs, but coming home from his second job, he found the demand greater than ever. Charlene still needed things fixed and sought help with the children. The lawn still needed mowing, and Charlene began to complain that their two-bedroom house was not large enough for their family.

Life, once so pleasant for Phil, rapidly became intolerable. He tried to escape by watching television and reading the newspaper, but that didn't work well because Charlene could still make him get up and help around the house. Next, he started staying after quitting time and hanging around with some of his co-workers, but that only aroused Charlene's ire. She felt hurt and angry when he wasn't coming home in time to help. When they sat down to talk with each other, which wasn't very often, Charlene used the opportunity to express her intense dissatisfaction with his lack of help with their children and household tasks. And when he came home from work late, which was almost always, Charlene was in no mood to make love with him. Eventually, he stopped coming home altogether.

Janet, a co-worker, wasn't at all like Charlene. When Phil talked with her, he could relax because she had no complaints, and she was not just willing, but eager, to make love whenever they could.

When I interviewed Phil, I learned that Janet was the single parent of six children. Phil would stop by her place about midnight, after he got off his second job. Janet's kids would be in bed, and a delicious steak dinner awaited him—along with the royal treatment. After dinner, they made love and went to sleep. Janet geared everything to provide for Phil's relaxation and pleasure.

This pattern persisted for months, with Phil never going back home. His wife, both furious and desperate, attempted to win him back by going to his office once in a while in the middle of the day to have sex with him. But she did not make much progress, because she felt too furious to give Phil the warmth and affection he got from Janet. In addition, the stress she underwent became so great that it seriously affected her health.

When Phil and I talked, I told him, "If you were single, you would never look twice at Janet. She's overweight, unattractive, and has six kids! She's not at all your type."

"But I love her," he protested. "I've never loved a woman so much in my whole life."

Eventually Charlene couldn't take it anymore and stopped trying to save her marriage. As soon as she gave up and let Phil know that she planned to divorce him, his affair with Janet began to fall apart. I knew it would, because Janet had provided a service in competition with Charlene. When that competition with Charlene no longer existed, much of Janet's motivation was lost. Besides, Janet had provided a degree of service no woman would sustain indefinitely. Janet thought she had Phil hooked and decided that now *she* deserved some of the royal treatment. The midnight steak dinners ceased, and Janet started making demands on Phil and giving him a taste of what being around her six kids felt like.

Phil backed out. He stopped seeing Janet, and after months of missing his family, he went back to Charlene. They worked together toward the goal of reuniting, and their relationship improved tremendously once Charlene could understand Phil's need for what I call "domestic support." I also worked with Phil and Charlene on their budget and helped them cut living expenses so Phil could work only one job. Phil was glad to help out at home, and with only one job to do, he picked up many of the chores Charlene had felt he neglected. At the same time, however, Phil desperately needed to feel that his wife handled the household and the children in an organized and efficient way. Charlene had been unwilling to assume the responsibilities of the home and had instead overemphasized her demands that Phil share the load. With all the hours Phil had to spend earning a living, Charlene's demands had seemed overwhelming. That motivated him to make the worst decision of his life—to begin a relationship with Janet.

Domestic Bliss—a Man's Fantasy

Unmet emotional needs often trigger fantasies, and the need for domestic support is no exception. A man's fantasy goes something like this: His home life is free of stress and worry. After work each day, his wife greets

145

him lovingly at the door and their well-behaved children are also glad to see him. He enters the comfort of a well-maintained home as his wife urges him to relax before having dinner, the aroma of which he can already smell wafting from the kitchen.

Conversation at dinner is enjoyable and free of conflict. Later the family goes out together for an early evening stroll, and he returns to put the children to bed with no hassle or fuss. Then he and his wife relax and talk together, watch a little television, and, at a reasonable hour, go to bed to make love.

Some wives may chuckle as they read the above scenario, but I assure you that if there is a wide gap between the reality of your home life and this fantasy, your marriage may be in serious trouble. A revolution in male attitudes toward housework is supposed to have taken place, with men pitching in to take an equal share of the household chores. But this revolution has not necessarily changed their emotional needs. Many of the men I counsel still tell me in private that they need domestic support as much as ever.

If behavior is any measure of attitude change, I don't see much change in the way men really feel about housework. They may talk a lot about how unfair it is to expect women to do most of the chores, but when it comes to actually sharing the burden, their wives know that it's mostly talk.

In the last chapter, I proposed a test to determine if women married men for their money. Would they marry a man who refused to earn an income? I've found that most men would marry a woman they love, even if she let him know unequivocally that he could not expect her to contribute to the family budget (I'm included in that group). Most women, on the other hand, would not marry a man who expected to be unemployed throughout his lifetime.

Technically, that test can be given to determine the existence of any basic emotional need. Would you have married your spouse knowing that he or she would be unwilling to provide any affection to you? How about sex? Or intimate conversation? Or honesty and openness? Add to that the caveat that whatever it is, you can't get it outside of marriage either—your spouse is the only ethical source. What can you do without? Whatever it might be, it's not a basic need for you.

So this test can be given to determine the need for domestic support. How many men would marry a woman who would refuse to manage housework or childcare? "When we marry and have children, don't expect me to be in charge of cooking the meals, cleaning the house, or diapering the baby," she would say just prior to the wedding vows.

I've counseled couples when the wife has taken this position. The husband is responsible for the housekeeping and child care. My experience with such couples is that this arrangement doesn't work, because the husband has a need for domestic support. He needs his wife to manage the home.

Time again for a disclaimer. Not all couples fit this pattern. I'm sure there are some couples who are happy with his caring for the children and managing the home. It's up to you to discover your basic emotional needs and then communicate them to each other. You may find that this need simply isn't an issue for you, and it may be that your wife has this need. That can happen.

You may object to my test by arguing that domestic support isn't an all-or-nothing proposition. It isn't something that only one person should do. It should be something done together. I heartily agree. I propose the test simply as a way for me to demonstrate the existence of a need. My point is that most men would have a very difficult time living with a wife who does little or no child care or housework. Women, on the other hand, may find such a husband frustrating, but it wouldn't necessarily ruin their marriage. In fact, many women in very successful marriages complain about their husband's unwillingness to help out more around the house.

The Fair Division of Labor Dilemma

Fifty years ago, it wasn't too difficult for the average wife to meet her husband's need for domestic support. That's because she was a full-time homemaker. But things have changed. Today the average wife is employed full-time. As would be expected, the division of domestic responsibilities has become a major source of marital conflict. Not only is she unable to meet her husband's need for domestic support, but now she senses that need herself. The "man's fantasy" that I described in the last section has become the "woman's fantasy" as well. They both want to relax after a stressful day at work.

Is the need for domestic support deep-seated and instinctive for men or is it driven by the demands of a career? Do women, who are exhausted by the demands of their career, feel the same need for domestic support as their husband?

Consider this common situation. The husband and wife both return home from work at about six and eat a take-out dinner with their two children. There are a few dishes to clean up, laundry to be washed and ironed, carpets to be vacuumed, children to be bathed, and stories to be read to them before they go to sleep. As soon as dinner is over, the husband sits down to watch TV.

Why doesn't the wife sit down with him and ignore the dishes, the laundry, the carpets, and the children? It's because she can't do it. She feels compelled to care for her home and her children. While he is in bed by ten, she is still up at midnight getting clothes ready for the children for the next day. She begs him for help, but he seems completely oblivious to her need.

If you are a full-time homemaker, it should not be too much of a problem for you to meet your husband's need for domestic support. By the time your husband comes home from work, your household tasks can be completed. You might want him to give you some help with the children, but after they're in bed, you're able to give him your undivided attention.

But if you have a full-time career, I'm sure that you have had to face the fair division of labor dilemma. You find yourself exhausted trying to do it all and you're very resentful that your husband doesn't provide more help.

There is almost unanimous agreement that both a husband and wife should share household and child care responsibilities if they both work full-time. But the wife's compulsion to care for the home and children, combined with the husband's need for domestic support, can easily get in the way of a fair division of labor. She wants domestic tasks completed, and he has a need for her to complete them. With these realities facing the average dual-career couple, how can they come to a fair division of labor?

When it comes to making any behavioral change, motivation is almost everything. If the change is enjoyable to the one who makes it, or if there is a reward for making the change, you can safely assume "mission accomplished." But if the change is unpleasant, and if there is no reward, all the promises to change will ultimately lead to broken promises.

With these motivational realities in mind, I've designed a way for dual-income couples to apply tried and proven motivational principles to solve their fair division of labor dilemma. If a wife wants help with domestic responsibilities from a husband with a need for domestic support, she should take the following steps.

Step 1: Identify Your Household Responsibilities

First, make a list of all of your household responsibilities, including child care. The list should (1) name each responsibility, (2) briefly describe what must be done and when to accomplish it, (3) name the spouse who wants it accomplished, and (4) rate how important it is to that spouse (use a scale from 0 to 5, with 0 indicating no importance and 5 indicating most important).

Both spouses should work on this list, and it will take several days to think of everything. You will add items each day as you find yourself accomplishing various tasks or wanting them accomplished.

Each time a task is added to the list and the work is described, the spouse wanting it done must be named along with his or her rating of the task's importance. But the other spouse must also consider to what extent he or she would want it accomplished. So the names and importance ratings of both spouses should eventually accompany each item.

Examples of items on the list are as follows:

Washing the breakfast dishes—clearing off the breakfast table every morning; washing, drying, and putting away all the breakfast dishes and utensils that went into preparing breakfast—Becky (4); John (2).

Feeding the cat—put cat food and water in the cat's dishes at 8:00 a.m. and 5:00 p.m.—John (5); Becky (0).

When you have finished your list, both of you should be satisfied that it includes all of the housekeeping and child care responsibilities that you share. You may have as many as a hundred items listed. Just this part of the exercise alone will help you understand what you're up against with regard to the work that you feel must be done.

Step 2: Assume Responsibility for Some Tasks

Now, each person must assume responsibility for tasks that you would enjoy doing or prefer doing yourself. Make two new lists, one list titled "His Responsibilities" and the other titled "Her Responsibilities." Then select items for which you are willing to take full responsibility. These are tasks that you would enjoy doing, don't mind doing, or want to do yourself so they can be done a certain way. When you have added an item to one of the two new lists, cross it off the original list.

If both you and your spouse want to take responsibility for the same items, you can either take turns doing them or arbitrarily divide them between the two of you. But you must approve each other's selections before they become that spouse's final responsibility. If one of you does not feel that the other will perform the task well enough, you might give each other a trial period to demonstrate competence. Once you have taken responsibility for any item, your spouse should be able to hold you accountable for doing it according to his or her expectations.

Now you have three lists: (1) the husband's list of responsibilities, (2) the wife's list of responsibilities, and (3) the list of household tasks that neither of you wants to do.

Step 3: Assign the Remaining Tasks

You are motivated to complete the tasks on your individual lists of responsibilities because you enjoy doing them or prefer to do them. But you are not as motivated to complete the remaining tasks. So to whom should they be assigned?

You may question my recommendation, but I suggest that these tasks be assigned to the person who wants them done the most. It's a reasonable solution, since to do otherwise would force responsibility on the one who cares least about their completion.

At this point in my plan, most women react with alarm. "I know how this will turn out," they complain. "All the remaining tasks will end up on my list. My husband could care less about keeping our home neat and clean."

Wives who are employed full-time want these tasks completed but don't have the time or energy to complete them. So they want their husband, who is also tired at the end of the day, to share the load. From their perspective, it's a fair division of labor to divide these tasks equally. It's unfair for the wife to be engaged in a wide assortment of household and child care tasks while her husband surfs the web. Even though she's the one who wants the work done, she feels he should share responsibility for doing it.

As most wives have discovered by now, wanting a husband to take responsibility for tasks that wives want completed doesn't work. He doesn't do them because he's not motivated. She can call him irresponsible and lazy all she wants, but in the end, she either completes the tasks or they won't be done.

Telling your husband that it's his responsibility to do something that you want done isn't motivating. In reality, it's usually de-motivating. It's likely to lead to an argument rather than to the help an exhausted wife needs from her husband.

I want you to get the help you need from your husband, but the way you go about getting that help must motivate him. Trust me. I won't leave you burdened with a list of household tasks that allows you only three hours of sleep each night. On the contrary, my plan will give you a full eight hours. But the plan begins by assigning undesirable tasks to the one most motivated to do them—the one who wants them done most.

When responsibility of all household and child care tasks has been assigned to the husband and wife, the wife's list will typically be far longer. That's because the husband has a need for domestic support—he needs her to care for him by cooking, cleaning, washing, ironing, and all the other common household tasks that make a house a home. Just because she works full-time and doesn't have the time or energy to complete these tasks doesn't reduce his craving for her domestic care.

When a wife first sees her list of responsibilities, she will feel overwhelmed, especially when I add the condition that she must have eight hours of sleep every night. So I help her think of ways to shift some of the responsibility to hired help or to the children. The need for domestic support isn't necessarily met by actually doing the household tasks. It's met by seeing to it that they're done—managing the household.

With household management in mind, a wife who is employed full-time should do as few household tasks herself as possible. The most time-consuming and unpleasant tasks should be hired out. Deep cleaning of the home (carpets, bathrooms, and kitchen) can be completed once a week by a cleaning service. Ironing can be sent out once a week. The lawn can be mowed and snow shoveled by a yard maintenance service. Having someone mow and trim the lawn can turn a burdensome Saturday into an opportunity to enjoy the day with the family.

On a related subject, be sure that you do not assign your children tasks that both you and your spouse find too unpleasant to shoulder. It doesn't build character to give your kids jobs that you hate to do; it builds resentment. If you want your children to help around the house, have them choose tasks from your list of household responsibilities that they would enjoy doing. Make lists for them, as well as for you and your spouse. There will be plenty to keep them busy.

Shifting household tasks to hired help will obviously cause a shift in budget priorities. But it should be recognized that when a wife has a full-time job, she can't be expected to do all of the housework too. And, as we've already seen, a husband is unlikely to be much help in relieving her burden. Or is that really true? Steps four and five of my plan are designed to motivate a man with a need for domestic support to help his wife meet that need.

Step 4: Indicate How Happy You Would Be with Your Spouse's Help

Up to this point, the assignment of household responsibilities is fair. You are dividing them according to willingness to do them and according to desire to have them accomplished. It also meets the husband's need for domestic support.

But there's hardly a wife who doesn't want help with her responsibilities, and she wants that help from her husband. Trying to *force* him to help by being disrespectful or appealing to his guilt doesn't work because it's not motivational. But there's something else she can do that will motivate most husbands—she can show appreciation for his help.

Establishing her responsibility for the household tasks is essential if his help is to be genuinely appreciated. If she thinks that some household tasks are his responsibility, when he completes them, he's simply done his duty. Why express special appreciation for something that he's supposed to do?

But if she accepts the tasks as her responsibility, and he offers to help, she will be grateful for the assistance.

You already have one number assigned to each task—the importance of the task to each of you. Now I want you to assign one more number. This time write a number indicating how many love units you think would be deposited if your spouse were to help you or would do that task for you. Use a scale from 0 to 5, with 0 indicating that you would experience no pleasure and 5 indicating that you would experience maximum pleasure and would be eternally grateful.

Step 5: Help Where Your Effort Is Most Appreciated

If these ratings are accurate, it means that whenever you have helped with a task that was rated a 4 or 5 by your spouse, you will be depositing many love units. Your help will make your spouse happy and it will be appreciated.

If cooking dinner or ironing shirts or picking up socks makes Love Bank deposits, why not do these things? As a matter of fact, if meeting any of the emotional needs I've described in this book really does create the feeling of love, why would anyone resist doing them? This is not only an act of care, but an act of supreme wisdom. By doing for each other what is most appreciated, you will have what few marriages have, the feeling of love throughout your entire lives.

But let me repeat another important concept that I have mentioned earlier. Don't waste your time on needs of lesser importance. Put your energy into what deposits the most love units and ignore tasks that do nothing for your spouse's Love Bank.

Don't do housework or child care for your spouse if it is not appreciated. Remember, whatever's on your spouse's list is your spouse's responsibility, not yours. If your effort to relieve your spouse of a particular task really doesn't seem to have much effect on your spouse, don't waste your time. Put your effort into another task that gives you more bang for the buck.

Your spouse's response to your help should prove whether or not love units are being deposited. If your spouse thanks you when you perform the task and expresses his or her appreciation with affection, you know you are on the right track. But if your spouse ignores you after performing one of these tasks, love units are not being deposited for some reason. In that case go back to your spouse's original list of tasks and pick something else to do that has a greater impact.

Just because you decide to help your spouse with one of his or her responsibilities does not make it your responsibility. Actually, that's a very important way to look at meeting emotional needs in general. If meeting any emotional need is viewed as a responsibility, then it is not appreciated as much when it's met. Only when the meeting of emotional needs is seen as a gift—as an act of care—does it have the maximum impact on the Love Bank. If either you or your spouse takes the meeting of any emotional need for granted, the effect will tend to be diluted.

I must make one final point. If you suffer in an effort to help your spouse with a household task, you will never get into the habit of helping with that task. And deposits in your spouse's Love Bank will be offset by withdrawals from yours. So you must figure out a way to help your spouse without the loss of your own love units.

To summarize, when creating a plan for a fair division of household responsibilities, depositing the most love units and avoiding their withdrawal should be your guide. Assume household responsibilities that you enthusiastically accept or want accomplished more than your spouse does. Then a husband should help his wife with tasks on her list that she would appreciate the most, and he must do tasks that don't withdraw love units from his own Love Bank.

This approach to the division of household responsibilities guarantees your mutual care, especially when you feel like being uncaring. It prevents you from trying to gain at your spouse's expense and from trying to force your spouse into an unpleasant way of life with you. It points you in a direction that will give both of you happiness, fulfillment, and best of all, the feeling of love for each other.

Questions for Her

1. What do you think of the "fair division of labor" plan that's offered in this chapter? Would it help you organize household tasks and discuss the best ways to achieve them?

2. Do you feel that your husband expects too much of you or do you expect too much of yourself when it comes to completing household tasks?

3. How do you react to the idea of managing the household tasks rather than trying to do them all yourself or trying to force your husband to do some of them?

Questions for Him

1. Do you feel that the "fair division of labor" plan that's been proposed in this chapter is really fair? When you don't provide as much help as your wife would like, do you feel guilty? Do you feel household tasks should be her responsibility?

2. How does your wife try to motivate you to help her with household tasks? Does she use demands, disrespect, or anger? Or does she request help and then show appreciation?

3. Have you ever identified domestic support as an emotional need? How would you feel if your wife pampered you the way Janet pampered Phil?

To Consider Together

1. Discuss the ways you have burdened each other with responsibilities:
   a. With a standard of living that requires more time at work than you like.
   b. With children's activities that are more time-consuming than you anticipated.
   c. With church or volunteer work that takes time away from your family.
   d. With hobbies and recreational interests that take time and re-sources away from higher priorities.

2. If a need for domestic support has been identified, follow the plan in this chapter to create a "fair division of labor." Try it for a few weeks before you judge its value.

3. Discuss this statement taken from the chapter: "If meeting any emotional need is viewed as a responsibility, then it is not appreciated as much when it's met. Only when the meeting of emotional needs is seen as a gift—as an act of care—does it have the maximum impact on the Love Bank."

She Needs Him
to Be a Good Father—
Family Commitment

Ann and Terry met in their early thirties. Neither of them had been married before, and both felt ready to settle down. Their relationship was very good, with one exception: Terry had no use for Ann's parents. Ann felt bad about this but she knew other couples who had problems that seemed worse to her. She and Terry got along so well in every other area that she decided to try to live with the problem. *Maybe, in time, it will work itself out*, she told herself.

Terry's eagerness to get away from Ann's family dampened the wedding celebration considerably. Ann hardly had time to greet her relatives before her new husband whisked her away on the honeymoon trip.

During their first year of marriage, Ann tried to interest Terry in her family get-togethers, but to no avail. She soon learned that he would have little to do with his own parents, much less spend time with hers.

The problem didn't "work itself out," and, as their two children arrived, Ann realized that Terry's lack of family commitment extended to them as well. When they were only babies, Ann wrote it off as a typical male attitude. *He'll be more interested when they get older*, she thought.

But Terry didn't become more interested. He had little time for the children, and when they clamored for his attention, he became irritable. Finally, Ann quit hoping and admitted to herself that she had married a man who just wasn't family oriented. She worried about what would happen to the children—especially little Tommy, who really needed his dad.

Ann hated to admit it, but Terry's bachelor cousin, Drew, was a better father to her children than Terry was. Drew visited regularly on holidays and over some weekends. He was so good with the kids they called him Uncle Drew. Drew eventually became their favorite babysitter, especially when Terry and Ann went away overnight. Drew's popularity with Ann's children left her ambivalent. While she could see Drew becoming their "father" in a sense, and that worried her, she also found comfort in knowing her children received the male supervision and companionship they needed so badly.

One day, when Ann was shopping at lunchtime, she saw Drew. After a few moments of conversation, Drew said, "Look, why don't we get something to eat?"

"I'd love it!"

After they had placed their orders with the waiter, Drew asked, "Well, how are my kids?"

His tender concern brought tears to Ann's eyes. "I've never told you how I worry about them," she began. In a few minutes she had poured out all her fears and worries about Terry's lack of commitment to the family. She concluded by confessing, "Sometimes, Drew, I feel as if you act more like a parent to my children than Terry does."

Drew was embarrassed but still had to smile. "You know I love those little guys as if they were my own." He reached across the table and held Ann's hand. "Look, I want to help. I'll start making a point to drop by more often to see them. How about if I take them to the county fair on Saturday?"

"That would be wonderful!" Ann beamed. "I might even come along myself."

Ann did go to the fair with Drew and the kids that Saturday. It began a steady pattern in which Drew earnestly sought to help compensate for his cousin's lack of commitment to his family. Terry did not seem to mind. He trusted Drew as a good friend as well as a member of the family.

Over the two years that followed that lunch, Ann and Drew began to see more and more of each other. They met often for lunch in addition to sharing outings with the children.

Ann began to admit to herself that she needed Drew in her life. He supported her in what seemed to be her most important responsibility— the care and development of her children. Slowly, over the months, their friendship became an affair. She came to love him with greater intensity and passion than she had ever loved any man.

The conflict that developed in Ann was unbearable. On the one hand, she did not want her children to go through the pain of divorce and be separated from their true father; on the other hand, she could not bear raising her children without the support of a man she loved.

Ann struggled with her emotions until Terry discovered the affair. He felt hurt and angry that his own cousin would betray him. To avoid the wrath of Terry and the rest of his family, Drew moved to another state. Now Ann felt doubly devastated. Her lover, and the man who had acted as a father to her children, was gone. Where would she go from here?

A Wife Needs a Strong Family Unit

Affairs like Ann and Drew's are not common but they do happen. I have counseled several couples like Ann and Terry, and every situation repeatedly impresses on me the wife's strong need for a family unit. Despite the current trend among many young couples to avoid having children, I still believe that the vast majority of women have a powerful instinct to create a family. Above all, wives want their husband to take a leadership role in their family and to commit himself to the moral and educational development of the children. The ideal scenario for a wife is to marry a man she can look up to and respect and then have her children grow up to be like their father.

In the Bible, Jewish parents were advised: "Train a child in the way he should go, and when he is old he will not turn from it" (Prov. 22:6). Whatever their religious convictions may be, most of the wives I counsel have no trouble seeing the wisdom in these words. They also expect their husband to play a key role in "training the children."

Women seem to know instinctively what we psychologists have discovered in research and practice: a father has a profound influence on his children. My own father exerted a powerful influence on my educational and moral development. He may not have known it at the time, because I often disagreed with him on many issues. On reaching adulthood, however, I found myself leaning toward his views more often than not. This development of my own moral values was extremely important to my mother, and she gave him a great deal of credit for training me in the way she wanted me to go.

In families where the father takes little interest in his children's development, the mother tries desperately to motivate him to change. She buys him books on parenting and leaves them in convenient places. She coaches him to attend seminars sponsored by the church or PTA. She may even ask him to talk with a family counselor in the hope that he can be inspired to greater interest and commitment. Her efforts usually meet with only partial success. More often she becomes frustrated by excuses, delays, and other unenthusiastic responses on her husband's part. Not uncommonly, such a mother starts looking to other men in her family or circle of friends to meet her need. She must have a man contributing to the well-being of her children. Sometimes a grandfather does the trick; other times a man like Drew appears and takes the place of the father with the children—and the place of the woman's husband as her lover.

What does a woman really mean when she says she wants her children to "have a good father"? Behind that remark lie expectations of responsibilities she wants him to fulfill. Ironically enough, they may conflict with his need for domestic support, which we considered in the last chapter. To deal with such a situation, the couple must achieve open communication in two important areas: time and training.

Parenting Takes Time—*Lots of Time*

A man should devote time to his family. He can strengthen both his marriage and his ties with his children by developing what I call "quality family time." This is not to be confused with child care tasks—feeding, clothing, and watching over children to keep them safe. Those are domestic tasks that were discussed in the last chapter. Quality family time is when the family is together for the moral and educational development of the children.

I have already recommended that a husband and wife schedule fifteen hours each week for giving undivided attention to each other. That time is to be spent meeting each other's intimate emotional needs so that their romantic love for each other remains strong. When I made that recommendation, you probably thought it couldn't be done, but with a goal of keeping your marriage secure, you may have found a way to schedule the time. If so, you have rearranged your priorities, spending your precious time on what means the most to you.

But now I will make a second recommendation that will require another rearrangement of priorities. I recommend an additional fifteen hours a week for quality family time. Without a doubt, the hours spent with your children are some of the most important hours of the week. And if you want to influence your children, training them to become successful adults, time together is crucial. But do you actually have that much time left in your schedule?

Consider your total time each week. You have 168 hours (24 hours a day, 7 days a week). For 8 hours of sleep each night (don't risk your health), take 56 hours away, leaving 112 hours. If you estimate the time it takes to get ready for work in the morning and ready for bed at night to take another 12 hours, that leaves 100 hours. Your job, including getting there and returning home again, should not take more than 50 hours a week (if you work more than that, you cannot achieve your most important objectives in life). After carving away time for all of these things, there are still 50 hours left for you to schedule. You have 15 hours for undivided attention and another 15 hours for quality family time, leaving you 20 hours for everything else you want to accomplish: household tasks, hobbies, church activities, more time at work, or just sitting at home relaxing.

A time budget (weekly schedule) is like a financial budget. It helps keep your priorities straight. If you don't budget your money, you will make so many low-priority purchases that you will have no money left for things that are truly important to you. The same is true with a time budget. If you don't schedule your week with your highest priorities in mind, you'll run out of time before you can accomplish them.

To make this change for your family, you will need to eliminate some activities that are currently in your schedule. But ask yourself, are the activities you will be eliminating more important than your care for each other and your care for your children?

Once you've carved out the hours in your schedule, you'll be ready to consider what you will be doing during this time. Remember, the purpose of quality family time is the moral and educational development of your children. Among the most important lessons to be taught are thoughtfulness and how to care for each other. So your activities should focus attention on helping each other, showing a cooperative spirit. Keep your family together as a unit during this time and make it fun for your children, not a time of drudgery.

What should you be doing during quality family time? Consider activities such as these:

- meals together as a family
- going out for walks and bike rides
- attending church services
- family meetings
- playing board games together
- reading to the children before bedtime
- helping the children with financial planning
- family projects and household tasks (be certain these are fun for the children, working on them together as a family)

You may find that making room in your schedule for quality family time doesn't really require the elimination of activities, but rather their modification. For example, if your family currently has meals on the run, with everyone grabbing a bite to eat separately, start having your meals together. Instead of activities that separate your family members, try to arrange to do things as a family. One of the biggest consumers of parental time is sports leagues. Can athletic activities be planned that keep the family together?

If you have children under the age of twelve, you will find it fairly easy to motivate them to spend time with you in this way. Once they reach their teens, however, they will begin to tax your ingenuity. Now they want to spend most of their time with their friends; your family begins to see less and less of them. To compensate, develop well-planned events aimed at teens; otherwise they will express their dissatisfaction clearly and with great vigor!

If your children have grown up with such family time, it should not be too difficult to get them to continue the practice. That doesn't mean you will not be challenged by teens who have other plans; but with some more thought and perhaps more expense in your plans, you can develop something your teens will *agree* to continue.

If you try to start family time during your children's teen years, they may not agree at all to such an arrangement. I've witnessed such heated arguments on this issue between parents and children that I have recommended that the family forget about quality family time; they have simply, though sadly, lost their opportunity.

Most educators realize that children are easier to influence than teens or adults. Take a page from their book, and if your children are still young, make the most of your ability to mold them with quality moral standards and life principles that can benefit them for years. Keep in mind the goal of training your child "in the way he should go," with his future needs in mind. If you take family time seriously in your children's early growth stages, you will not find yourself in trouble later.

Parenting Takes Training—*Lots of Training*

If you wish to parent your children well, you also need to face the fact that you will need some training in this skill. No one is born knowing how to care for a child.

Terry, Ann's husband, didn't believe training would do him any good. He knew he was a terrible father, so he avoided spending time with his children. His cousin, Drew, seemed to know what to do, so Terry let him take over. But only Terry could be the real father. If only Terry had realized that he *could* learn the skills he needed. Just as with any skill, he could improve by reading good books on parenting or taking some classes. A little practice is all it would have taken. Both he and his children would have enjoyed their time together. As a grand prize, Terry would also have met one of his wife's basic needs.

Hundreds of books on parenting appear on bookstore and library shelves each year, and countless seminars try to explain how to train children. These resources abound with information on everything from toilet training to enforcing bedtimes. But the following are a few basic guidelines for fathers that most mothers would enthusiastically endorse.

1. Learn How to Reach Agreement with Your Wife

From an emotional needs standpoint, it makes no sense for a father to ignore his wife's opinions regarding child training. She needs him to join her in the educational and moral development of their children—not take over completely. But many fathers don't know how to negotiate with their wife. They think conflicts in child training must be decided by force—which parent is strong enough to get his or her way? If his wife prevails, he steps back and lets her train the children by herself. If he prevails, he wants her to submit to his authority.

I've found that the wisest approach to child training is found through negotiation that leads to a mutually enthusiastic agreement. If a mother and father agree on the rules their children will be expected to follow and agree on how to discipline them when those rules are not followed, they avoid the common mistakes most parents make. And the wife's need for family commitment is met.

If they can get away with it, children learn to divide and conquer. They make a deal with Mom to get around Dad. To avoid that age-old strategy, when a child wants a privilege, both Mom and Dad should consult in private and give an agreed-on answer.

In family after family, I have witnessed children successfully manipulate one parent who favors them. Father favors Monika; mother favors Jennifer. So Monika goes to father for money, and he tries to give it to her without mother knowing. When Jennifer finds out about it, she demands the same treatment. Mother tries to make father give Jennifer the same amount of money, resulting in a deep wedge driven between husband and wife. To avoid this, all decisions *must* result from mutual agreement. If you cannot agree, take *no* action.

Reach agreement too on how you want to discipline your children. A joint opinion receives greater respect from children and carries more weight with them. When they know you made it together, children are less likely to challenge your decision.

How a husband disciplines his children greatly affects his deposits in his wife's Love Bank. Women are very sensitive to inappropriate and overly harsh discipline. Often they react as if the punishment the husband gives their children had been given to them personally. Therefore he should reach an enthusiastic agreement with his wife before imposing a disciplinary solution. A method of discipline that a husband and wife plan and implement jointly builds her love for him and reflects his care for her feelings.

2. Learn How to Explain the Rules

Children need to understand *why* they should do this or that. Men especially should learn how to clearly and patiently explain the rules. Sometimes the conversation may go like this:

"Johnny, go upstairs and make your bed."

"Why?"

"Because we want you to grow up knowing how to keep yourself and your property neat and clean."

"Why?"

"Because being neat and clean makes the people you live with feel good and like living with you."

"Why?"

"Just go upstairs and make your bed *BECAUSE I SAID SO!*"

"Oh, okay."

You can easily understand the father's reaction to those seemingly endless questions, can't you? But the "because I said so" line doesn't benefit the child very much. When you feel frustrated, pulling out your parental muscle may work—you may get the child to take the appropriate action—but you may also have lost the opportunity to explain your rationale to the child. In situations such as these, you can subtly but clearly communicate your moral, ethical, and personal values, if you patiently answer the *whys*.

3. Learn How to Be Consistent

Children don't take long to discover that rules may depend on Daddy's mood. When he feels happy, they can do almost anything—run around the house, throw things, jump on the beds, yell at each other, and have a squirt-gun fight. When he comes home grumpy, watch out! Movement of any kind will be met with an angry outburst.

If rules are applied inconsistently, their meaning is lost to children. Instead of learning a moral principle, Daddy's mood becomes the focus of their attention. It only becomes wrong for Johnny to yell at the top of his lungs when Daddy needs to concentrate on something or doesn't feel up to par. Parents should make rules together and then stick to them, regardless of their mood.

4. Learn How to Punish Properly

Many children whose parents *never* spank them run wild. But corporal punishment should be used only in very early years (no later than age seven) and should be used to send a message, rather than inflict physical pain. A spank that doesn't leave a mark can get the point across when children are very young.

But when children are between the ages of eight and twelve, noncorporal punishment is more appropriate and far more effective. Taking away privileges is the time-honored way parents punish older children. Incentives for good behavior should begin to replace punishment for bad behavior when training this age group.

By the time a child becomes a teenager, punishment should be completely phased out in favor of incentives. Some well-meaning parents punish their teenagers by taking away some of their basic rights and doing things such as grounding them, only to have them run away or even attempt suicide. Corporal punishment that is inflicted on older children can leave an emotional scar that persists throughout their lives.

The very best way to train your children is by example. As you demonstrate your care for each other by meeting each other's basic needs, and by protecting each other from your selfish habits, your children will learn what it means to be thoughtful. The quality family time you spend with your children, teaching them important values, such as to consider each other's feelings before acting, will go a long way toward raising children who need little or no punishment.

5. Learn How to Handle Anger

Often parents discipline their children in a state of anger. When they've had quite enough of a child's disobedience, they let loose. Just the other day, I witnessed an example of such behavior in a shopping center parking lot. Inside the store, a child was kicking and screaming because his mother would not buy him a toy. The ruckus continued through the checkout line and all the way to their car. But after the mother had left the watchful eyes of guards and surveillance cameras, she began beating her son mercilessly. She wanted to let him know what a big mistake he had made, and I'm sure he got the message. But was it the right way for her to train her son?

An angry outburst is temporary insanity, and the damage it can do is dangerous and unpredictable. If you were to watch a video recording of one of your angry outbursts, you'd see my point. But that's precisely what your children view when you use anger to punish them—they see an insane parent.

Even if angry outbursts were an effective means of punishment, they'd be far too risky to use with children. Broken bones, permanent injury, and even death are the all too-common consequences of this sad measure of discipline.

But discipline accompanied with anger doesn't usually work. Consider the disobedient child I witnessed in the store. I'm sure that his mother had beaten him many times before that incident. It wasn't working. That's because discipline given in anger is not carefully planned. It's impulsive and it teaches a child that an angry outburst is an appropriate way to vent frustrations.

No child psychologist I have ever studied has recommended anger in any form as a tool for training a child. Control your anger *before* you discipline any child. By separating your emotion from the disciplinary action, you will become a far more effective disciplinarian.

Don't Let Parenting Compete with Romance

A common complaint I hear from new fathers is that the lover they married has been transformed into a mother. What they mean is that their wife has lost interest in romance. This is easy for a mother to do when overwhelmed with the new responsibility of raising a child. But it can be avoided if time for undivided attention is scheduled throughout a couple's child-rearing years.

Affairs are extremely common when a couple has their first child. Divorce is also more likely to occur during that year. Isn't that sad? The cause for these tragic events is usually a couple's failure to meet each other's basic needs. The priority of parenting competes with the priority of romance, and parenting wins.

When a wife is transformed from a lover into a mother, most men see only their loss of sexual fulfillment and recreational companionship as factors in their marital collapse. But what can also happen is that her needs for affection and intimate conversation are also unmet. Their loss of privacy and time to give each other undivided attention prevents him from meeting her most basic needs. Even if he becomes a good father, taking an active role in their child's personal development, it doesn't compensate for his failure to meet her intimate emotional needs. So when women want their husband to spend every free moment caring for their children, if they ignore their own need for undivided attention, they run a very high risk of falling out of love with him.

It's so important for parenting and romance to coexist in marriage that I've written *His Needs, Her Needs for Parents* to help couples balance their desire to be good parents with their need for intimacy. In it I explain more fully many of the points I've made in this chapter. If you are new parents or are contemplating becoming parents, I highly recommend this book to you.

Questions for Him

1. Have you committed yourself to your family? What does this mean in regard to quality family time and training in parenting skills?
2. Are you experiencing any problems with anger, administering punishment, consistency, or agreement with your wife on child discipline?
3. Are you overcome with responsibilities? How have you tried to communicate your juggling act to your wife? Does she seem to understand?

Questions for Her

1. Does your role as a mother interfere with your role as a wife? Has your husband ever complained about it?
2. Have you tried to encourage your husband to play a greater role in the moral and educational development of your children? If so, has it been effective? What could be more effective?
3. Have you and your husband made an effort to educate yourselves in parenting skills? What parenting problems that you face could use some attention?

To Consider Together

1. Share your answers to the above questions with each other honestly but respectfully.
2. What are the educational and moral goals you have for your children? Are you in agreement? How should your children be disciplined? Are you in agreement?
3. Schedule fifteen hours for quality family time. Plan activities during this time that help you achieve the educational and moral goals you have for your children. But don't let it interfere with the time you schedule to give undivided attention to each other.

He Needs Her 12
to Be Proud of Him—
Admiration

"Oh, Charles, thank you." Lori's eyes lit up with excitement. "What a wonderful painting! No one ever gave me his own original artwork before. You have so much talent."

"I don't know about that, Lori. I've got a long way to go."

"You underestimate yourself, honey. You are really good. I know enough about art to know that. You always do such fine work. You're a great artist, and I'm proud of you."

In Charles and Lori's courtship days, that would have been a typical snatch of conversation. She forever heaped praise on him, and it felt great. He'd never been complimented like that before.

After they married, Lori's remarks gradually started to change. Charles, contented with his job in commercial design, seemed altogether too relaxed about his career to suit her. She wanted him to become a famous artist. As she began to feel convinced he would never develop his potential, Lori's words of admiration tapered off and then ended altogether.

Meanwhile, at the studio, Charles found himself teamed more often with Linda. She showed a knack for layout and graphics, and together they came up with some winning displays. One day as they shared lunch, Charles started to unburden himself to her. "You know, Linda, I think my wife is right. I haven't done much to develop my career in art. I'm too lazy."

"Lazy!" Linda protested. "How could she think that? Does she know how tough this business is? Why, I can't think of *anyone* your age who has gone farther than you as an artist. Your wife just doesn't understand what it takes. Besides, you're one of the nicest men I've ever met. She should feel lucky she married someone as wonderful as you."

Charles hardly knew what to say. "Thanks, Linda," he finally managed. "It's really kind of you to say that."

"It's not just kindness. I meant it."

Charles savored the compliment all day. Finally, someone appreciated him for what he was right now, not for what he could become someday. It felt good to live up to someone's expectations for a change.

Not long after, Charles and Linda began their affair. When the president of their company discovered it, he referred Charles and Lori to me for marriage counseling.

Why This Male Need for Admiration?

One of the principles I taught Lori was that honest admiration is a great motivator for most men. When a woman tells a man she thinks he's wonderful, that inspires him to achieve more. He sees himself as capable of handling new responsibilities and perfecting skills far above those of his present level. That inspiration helps him prepare for the responsibilities of life.

Not only does admiration motivate, it also rewards the husband's existing achievements. When his wife tells him that she appreciates him for what he has done, it gives him more satisfaction than he receives from his paycheck. A woman needs to appreciate her husband for what he already is, not for what he could become if he lived up to her standards.

For some men, admiration also helps them believe in themselves. Without it these men seem inherently more defensive about their shortcomings.

Often they hate to see a counselor, because they do not want someone to be critical of them. Many have come to me in the guise of helping their wife "with her emotional problems."

While criticism causes men to become defensive, admiration energizes and motivates them. A man expects—and needs—his wife to be his most enthusiastic fan. He draws confidence from her support and can usually achieve far more with her encouragement.

Confidence Usually Begins at Home

Poor self-confidence, a common problem for both men and women, begins very early—in the home, during childhood. The man with a low opinion of his ability has probably had friends and family who criticized and complained about his failings, and he has expected others to continue that critical pattern. In particular he expects his wife to pick up where his parents left off and continue to remind him of his shortcomings and failures.

In such cases I advise clients to reject these negative evaluations and I encourage them to surround themselves with friends and relatives who see their value and accomplishments. Many times such a change does the trick, and within weeks their confidence improves measurably. An environment of carping and criticism is dangerous to your mental health, whereas those who support and encourage you bring out your true potential and spark your genius.

In my own life, I've seen the powerful effect of admiration through the blessing of an admiring grandmother. As a small child I remember vividly her telling me that I was a genius and more talented than anyone in the whole world. Although that somewhat misguided belief created some social problems for me in kindergarten, her attitude toward me also placed within me the seeds of confidence.

Once in high school, a counselor reviewed my grades and other test scores and concluded I could never succeed in college and should seriously consider skilled labor. Thanks to my grandmother's contradictory viewpoint, I went to college anyway, did much better than the counselor expected, and went on to earn a doctorate degree. Without my grandmother's admiring opinion, I might have agreed with my counselor and failed to gain the benefit of that education.

You've heard the saying, "Behind every great man is a great woman." I'd like to amend it to make Harley's Fifth Corollary:

Behind every man should be an admiring wife.

Biographies of great men prove it, and lives of all men show it: a man simply thrives on a woman's admiration. To a great extent men owe gratitude to their wives for this kind of emotional support, for without it, their confidence, the major source of their success, can erode and eventually crumble.

Criticism versus Complaints

If one of a man's basic emotional needs is admiration, I think you can understand why so many marriage experts have warned wives to avoid criticizing their husband. Criticism is the opposite of admiration.

A man wants his wife to be president of his fan club, not his worst critic, but some women feel that it's their right and obligation to "straighten out" their husband. So instead of showering him with accolades, they batter him with disapproval.

In my book *Love Busters*, I describe disrespectful judgments as one of the ways that spouses destroy their love for each other. Instead of making massive Love Bank deposits with admiration, spouses make massive withdrawals with criticism.

Please understand, I do not recommend sweeping marital problems under the rug. I'd be the first to encourage spouses to express their grievances to each other. But to do it disrespectfully is ineffective and very damaging to a relationship, especially if a spouse has a need for admiration.

I draw a distinction between a criticism and a complaint. A complaint is the expression of a problem that you would like to solve. For example, "I have been feeling sexually frustrated lately and I'd like to make love to you more often." This is a complaint.

A criticism, on the other hand, adds disrespect to the complaint. "You have certainly been a disappointment to me. I had no idea you would turn out to be such a lousy lover." This changes the complaint into a criticism.

Which of the two expressions of need has the greatest chance of succeeding? One places the problem on the docket for discussion and negotiation. The other sets the stage for a fight.

While admiration may be difficult to express honestly in a marriage where everything seems to be turning out badly, criticism can be completely eliminated by simply avoiding disrespectful comments. If you have a complaint, get it out on the table, but keep your criticisms to yourself.

A Plan to Create Greater Admiration

Before you begin trying to heap words of praise on your spouse, I should give you a word of caution. Never fake your admiration. By simply saying flattering words to your husband, you can do more harm than good. To have any value, praise must genuinely reflect your feelings. For example, when my grandmother told me she thought I was brilliant, she honestly believed it, and her conviction convinced me.

I can hear a lot of wives saying to themselves, *That's all well and good, Dr. Harley, but what if your husband is a constant source of irritation? What if he always fouls things up? How can I learn to admire a man like that?* These very important questions require thoughtful answers.

Sometimes a marriage can be so unsuccessful that spouses stop looking for the value in it. They want to get away from it so badly that they convince themselves there is nothing to respect in each other. But that's an illusion. The truth is that, regardless of the struggles you might be facing, there is value in everyone, even your spouse.

So I encourage the wife of a man with a need for admiration to start looking for value in him. As she thinks of what he does, his traits, and his characteristics, she begins to find things she genuinely admires about him. Writing them down as they occur to her helps her remember them and reflect on their value. It doesn't take long before she can express her honest admiration for some of her husband's strengths.

Of course, building a large inventory of admirable characteristics can be more difficult than finding a few things to admire and then learning to express appreciation for them. So I have designed a plan that helps a man give his wife more to admire. It requires him to do what I've been encouraging throughout this book—meet her most basic emotional needs.

You've seen how the Love Bank works, how learning to meet each other's basic needs creates the feeling of love. Well, the process of creating the feeling of respect in a woman works in a very similar way. As a husband learns to meet his wife's five most important needs, she finds herself responding with a natural and overflowing respect for him. Conversely, if a man does not meet these needs, she cannot in all honesty express the degree of admiration he needs from her. Therefore much of her admiration depends on his ability to meet her basic marital needs.

Keeping this observation in mind, my plan helps a man identify and meet his wife's basic needs.

Step 1: Identify Behaviors That Build or Destroy Admiration

A wife makes two lists, the first describing behaviors she admires in her husband, the second describing those that destroy her admiration. In both lists, she groups these items into the five basic need areas we have already considered for women.

As an example, we will look at a list Rachel made that evaluates her husband, John.

Behavior That I Admire	Behavior That Destroys My Admiration
Affection	*Affection*
1. Holds my hand when we're out together.	
2. Hugs me when he comes home from work.	
3. Sends me surprise cards and flowers.	
Conversation	*Conversation*
4. Talks to me about how his day went and how I spent mine.	1. When I feel upset, he buries himself in his work and won't talk to me.
5. Takes an interest in my daily activities and discusses them with me.	

176

Behavior That I Admire	Behavior That Destroys My Admiration
Financial Support	*Financial Support*
6. Earns a good income to support me and our children.	
Honesty and Openness	*Honesty and Openness*
7. Always tells me where he has been and leaves numbers where I can reach him in an emergency.	2. When something bothers him, he denies it, even though I can tell he's upset.
Family Commitment	*Family Commitment*
	3. He does not take enough time to be with me and our children together as a family.
	4. He does not discipline the children but leaves the training entirely to me.
	5. He never shows any interest in our children's activities and never attends PTA meetings.

The example above shows that John must begin to meet his wife's need for family commitment before she will be able to admire him completely. Their difficulty with conversation may also reflect on his failure in family commitment—Rachel becomes upset with his lack of interest in the children, and he will not talk about it. Since he already feels overextended and has no time for the children's projects, he feels that talking about it cannot help. If he learns to meet her need for family commitment, their conversation problems may disappear.

Step 2: Make a Trade

It is usually easier to overcome a marital problem when both husband and wife see the need to improve their ability to care for each other. He'll feel encouraged if he knows he's not the only one who needs to make changes and that his wife has to take some corrective action too. So from a practical standpoint, a wife will more successfully motivate her spouse to make changes in his behavior if she is willing to make a few alterations herself.

The wife should ask her husband to answer the same questions she's answered. What does she do for him that he admires, and what does she do that ruins his admiration of her?

177

Spouses need to prepare themselves for defensive reactions from each other when they read the lists. Remember these lists are not demands for change. They merely reflect what spouses can do for each other that will help create greater admiration.

When you have completed your lists, agree together to enhance behavior that builds admiration and overcome behavior that destroys admiration for either of you. Ideally, your trade-off should include *all* items you've listed. Once you've made your trade and are willing to address your spouse's grievances, you move on to the next step.

Step 3: Learn New Habits

There is a simple and straightforward method to form new habits:

1. Define the habit you want to form.
2. Create incentives for repeating the habit and disincentives for falling back into old habits.
3. Repeat the habit until it becomes almost effortless.

Let's see how it worked for John and Rachel. When they made up their lists, Rachel said that John's lack of interest in the activities of the children destroyed her admiration for him. After some thought, Rachel converted the statement, "interest in the activities of the children" into a habit, "spending five hours each week working with the children with any of their activities." She further refined her definition to consist of three parts:

1. Sunday night at 7:00, ask the children what activities they planned that week.
2. For each child, select one activity with which you will help.
3. Set aside five hours for these activities.

Every strategy must include incentives for following the new habit and disincentives for falling back into old habits. Together John and Rachel planned that she would watch *Monday Night Football* with him when he spent the five hours with the children; if he failed to do so, he agreed not to watch any sports on television that week.

178

The primary reason people have difficulty forming habits is that they don't repeat a behavior often enough. So John and Rachel agreed to practice for five months, August through December.

Once they announced the plan to the children, they were off to a running start. For eight weeks straight, John spent the time with the children. On the ninth week he slipped. He had many good reasons. He got sick and fell behind in his work, he had to repair the front door, and Rachel's sister dropped in for a two-day visit. Despite these good reasons, he gave up watching sports for the next week, and Rachel didn't have to watch football either.

The rest of the program went as planned, and at the end of December they evaluated his new habit to see if their strategy had worked. The indications seemed good. Not only did he now spend five hours with the children in their activities, he had begun to plan new ones with them, when he could help them even more. And Rachel found herself watching football even when John wasn't home.

When I work with couples on forming new habits, I warn them that they may find their first efforts disappointing. Their original plan to motivate enough repetition may need several revisions before it really works. Remember that repetition is the key to forming a new habit, and incentives are the key to guaranteeing repetition. A mere commitment to change won't get the job done if it's not accompanied by solid incentives to repeat the new behavior long enough for it to become a habit.

What's Next?

What should a wife do when she begins to admire her husband? Tell him, of course! However, this is not always as easy as it seems. You may not have developed the habit of telling your husband that you admire him. Just because you *feel* pride or admiration does not mean you communicate it. Teach yourself to speak those words of praise, just as you have learned any other habit.

At first, it may seem awkward, but as your habit develops, it will become smoother and more spontaneous. Then you will have achieved your goal—the natural admiration he's always wanted from you.

Sometimes a woman fears expressing praise too soon, because her husband might stop working on behavior that has not yet become habitual. But I advise her to communicate praise as soon as she feels even a *little* admiration—not just as a reward for change but as a true expression of her feelings.

Remember that most men really *need* appreciation. They thrive on it. Many men who come to me because they have had affairs stress that the admiration of their lover was like a warm spring breeze compared to the arctic cold of their wife's criticism. It was hard to resist. Don't tempt your husband to go outside your marriage for approval; he needs your appreciation.

Questions for Her

1. Has the expression of admiration toward your husband been a special problem for you? Has he ever asked you to be less critical of him or encouraged you to count your blessings?
2. Do you need to develop a feeling of admiration or simply the habit of expressing your admiration?
3. Make the list of changes in your husband that would make you a more admiring wife. Divide the list into essential changes and unessential changes. If your husband made the essential changes, would you be able to show him the admiration he needs?

Questions for Him

1. Are you aware of your need for admiration? Some men never give it a thought and don't think they need it. What evidence is there in your life that you may have a deep and basic need for your wife's praise?
2. How have you tried to communicate the need of admiration to your wife? How has she responded?
3. Make the list of changes in your wife that would make you a more admiring husband. Divide your list into essential changes and unessential changes. If your wife made these essential changes, would you be willing to make the changes your wife will suggest to you?

To Consider Together

1. What do you think of the plan suggested in this chapter? How might you modify it to make it more applicable to your marriage?
2. Develop incentives for changing the habits you've identified. Set a time limit on how long you will be practicing the new behavior and evaluate the change at the end of that time.
3. Practice admiring each other and avoid criticism. Learn to express your needs in the form of a request. For example, "How would you feel about helping me with a problem I've been having?"

How to Survive an Affair

13

Alex sighed quietly as he reached over to turn out the light. Then he turned back to kiss Jasmine's cheek. "Good night, honey," he whispered.

No answer. Jasmine was sound asleep. That did not surprise him, and he knew how angry she'd be if he woke her just to make love. He lay down and pulled the covers over his shoulder. Long ago he had given up the loser's game of feeling sorry for himself. He just had to face it that Jasmine no longer had any interest in sex. She used to, he'd thought, in the early years of their marriage, before the children came along.

Next morning as Alex caught the 7:30 commuter train, he greeted Heather and Brandon, who also worked for his firm. When Alex opened his morning paper, he remembered his empty noon schedule.

"Hey, you two," he called out. "My lunch partner's out of town today. Either of you free?"

"Sorry," Brandon told him, "I have to be across town."

Alex looked at Heather, a tall, willowy woman, studious and plain. "I'd love to go to lunch with you," she answered brightly.

I haven't seen her in a while, Alex thought. Heather had gone to his high school, and they'd lost track of each other for a few years, until they started working for the same company. Their friendship rekindled several months before, when they began working on the same team, installing a new computer system. Once they'd completed that, though, Alex's responsibilities took him to the fifth floor, while she stayed on the seventh.

"You know," Alex told her that day at lunch, "I'm kind of glad Charlie had to go out of town today."

"Me too," she agreed, smiling. "I've missed you since you went downstairs. We should have done this sooner."

"Yeah. Working on that project was the most fun I've had in a long time."

"The system's really proving itself too. Float time on orders has been reduced to almost nothing."

"That doesn't surprise me." Alex chuckled. "Why, with you and me on that job, it *couldn't* fail."

As they left the restaurant, Alex and Heather made plans to meet again next week. Soon the midweek lunch date had become a regular part of their schedules. Once Heather gave Alex a book on computer programming, and a few weeks later he responded with a modest but lovely bracelet. As he gave it to her at lunch, her face lit up. Leaning over the table, she kissed him gently on the cheek.

"Heather, I have to be honest," he told her awkwardly. "I'm getting awfully attached to you. It's . . . well, it's more than friendship."

"Alex," she responded, her voice low, "I feel that way too."

"I've never told you how I feel about Jasmine . . ."

"And you never need to," she reassured him.

"But I want to. I've never been able to talk to anyone about it before. I'd like to now."

"Then go ahead. It's okay."

"When I married her, I didn't realize what I was letting myself in for. I thought we shared a lot of interests, would spend a lot of time together, but all that dried up within a year or so. Now she does her thing, and I do mine. She doesn't like me to talk to her about work, and she complains I don't earn enough money. Half the time, when I get home at night, it's like walking into a madhouse."

Heather listened in sympathetic silence. After work he stopped by her place "to talk."

The next morning, when Alex awakened in Heather's bed, he thought how pretty she looked. He kissed her bare shoulder and smiled as she opened her eyes. "Hi, handsome," she whispered.

"Hello, beautiful."

After that evening, Alex and Heather seemed obsessed with each other. Never in his life had Alex experienced such enthusiastic and consistent lovemaking.

At first, Jasmine had only some vague doubts about Alex, but soon her doubts turned to suspicions as his absences increased. The occasional stay in town overnight extended to his leaving the house on weekend afternoons. Finally one night, she decided to test her suspicions and called Jake, with whom Alex said he planned to spend the night. Jake tried to say Alex hadn't arrived yet, but his hesitation left Jasmine unconvinced. When she tried to call later, no one answered the phone.

Jasmine remembered hearing Alex talk warmly about working with Heather on a computer project. She also knew Heather didn't live too far away and decided she might be a likely prospect. One Saturday afternoon when Alex had disappeared, Jasmine hired a neighborhood teenager to watch the children and drove to Heather's apartment. As soon as she turned onto her block, she spotted Alex's car, parked just around the corner.

Jasmine parked, found Heather's apartment, and took a deep breath as she rang the bell. Heather answered the door, wearing a dressing gown. "Jasmine!" she said just a bit too loudly. "Why, what a surprise . . ."

"I'm sorry, Heather, if this seems rude, but I must come in to see something for myself." She brushed past the other woman and walked through the apartment, into the bedroom. There she found Alex, hurriedly pulling on his trousers. The rest of his clothes were still draped over a chair near the bed.

"Jasmine! I—"

His wife spun around and walked out of the apartment without saying a word. She saw no signs of Heather and didn't even bother to close the door on her way out. Once in her car, Jasmine burst into tears. As she drove home, she attempted to force her numb mind to think. Divorce seemed her only option.

Alex and Heather stood by the front window and watched Jasmine drive away. "What will you do?" Heather asked.

"I've got to go after her and try to cool her down. Don't worry about it, love. It's going to work out."

When he got home, Alex saw Jasmine's car, engine running and door ajar, standing in the driveway. He turned off the ignition, pocketed the key, and closed the door. As he walked through the front door, he heard the children crying. The bewildered babysitter told him his wife had gone upstairs. He paid her and sent her home, then went to find Jasmine. She had locked herself in the bedroom. After calling to her a few times, he realized he'd better take care of the kids first. They went out for some fast food, and he put them to bed. All that time the door to the bedroom remained tightly shut.

Again Alex knocked at the door. No answer. "Jasmine, please," he begged softly.

The lock on the knob clicked, and he tried the door again. As it opened, he saw Jasmine sitting on the bed, eyes swollen from crying. He walked over to her. "I'm so ashamed, honey—"

"Don't you *dare* call me honey!" she hissed.

"But Jasmine, I love you and the children. You mean the world to me. I don't understand how I could have done this to you." Again Jasmine started sobbing, and instinctively Alex tried to comfort her.

"Don't touch me!" she gasped, struggling away from him to perch in the middle of the bed. "How could you do that? I hate the sight of you!"

"Jasmine, please . . . It'll never happen again. I must have been crazy. Please give me another chance." Tears welled up in his eyes.

"You liar! You lied to me about all those nights you had to spend at Jake's, didn't you!?"

"Jasmine, please, no—"

"Don't lie. It only makes it worse!"

"You're right, and I won't lie anymore. You've got to believe me! I can only promise you it won't happen again. You and the kids mean too much to me. It's all over, Jasmine. I mean it."

This sort of exchange continued until three o'clock in the morning—Alex begging Jasmine for mercy and understanding, and Jasmine ripping into him with rage and anguish. Finally, driven by exhaustion, she permitted a truce and allowed Alex to come to bed.

During the next few days, Alex continued to show remorse and managed to quiet Jasmine down somewhat. By the end of the week, he had her convinced that temporary insanity caused his fling with Heather and it wouldn't happen again.

Alex did stop seeing Heather for lunch but he called her at the first opportunity. "I've got to see you but I don't dare right now. I love you so much—I just don't know what to do."

"Alex, I love you too. There'll never be any question of that. But I want you to hold your marriage together. I don't want to cause a divorce."

"Heather, you're a jewel. Don't worry. I'll give it my best shot. If it ends in divorce, it won't be your fault."

Alex held out for two weeks and then rendezvoused with Heather for lunch at an out-of-the-way spot. "I can't stop thinking about you and what we have together. I've never had anything like it in my life and I know I won't ever have it again."

Heather could only hold Alex's hand and weep. The next week they met at Jake's apartment and resumed the affair with renewed vigor. It seemed as if they had new energy, stored up over the past weeks of separation. After that, they got together whenever possible for lunch. Staying in town overnight was out, because Jasmine would suspect. One Saturday afternoon, however, Alex couldn't stand it and quietly left for Heather's apartment. He didn't realize that Jasmine had seen him go and had followed. They repeated the whole sorry discovery scene, which left Jasmine utterly inconsolable. She ordered Alex out of the house and filed for divorce.

Alex thought about moving in with Heather but decided against it. Instead, he found a room to rent, where he sat and thought about what had happened. He realized not only that he missed Jasmine and the children, but that he had many other things to think about—being rejected by his family and friends and having to spend large sums of money on lawyers, alimony, and child support. He also thought about his company and their policy concerning affairs and keeping families together. He could lose his job—or at least miss an upcoming promotion.

One evening, about a week after he had moved out, Alex phoned Jasmine. "Please give me one more chance. I think our marriage was in trouble long before this thing happened. I know there were things I was trying to ignore and I was wrong to do that. I should have brought it all out in the open with you and a counselor. Jasmine, I really want to save our marriage and our family. Will you go to see someone with me?"

At first, Jasmine didn't know how to reply. Was Alex right? Maybe she was partly to blame. And he did want to see a counselor.

"Okay," she finally responded. "I'll give it a try."

Before the week was out, Alex had moved back home. He managed one brief conversation with Heather, telling her he still loved her but could not get a divorce—not yet, anyway.

During counseling sessions, Alex tried to explain his feelings about why he felt the marriage had gone wrong—and why he held resentment against Jasmine.

"Alex," said the counselor, "you need to spell out what you thought was wrong. Let's get specific."

Alex got specific and talked about Jasmine's indifference to having sex, her lack of interest in his career, and her unwillingness to share in activities he enjoyed. Then he cited the incessant nagging about household problems, even though she had never had to go out and get a job.

As Jasmine listened, she began to wonder if perhaps a lot of the problem wasn't really her fault after all.

Then the counselor zeroed in and asked Alex to be totally honest. Was he still in love with Heather?

"Yes, I am," Alex said in a mixture of shame and defiance. Alex didn't bother to say that he and Heather had resumed their affair and still spent lunch hours at Jake's apartment. The counselor did not ask.

In the following months Alex managed to remain in counseling and continue his affair with Heather. He fooled both Jasmine and the counselor into believing he was interested in being permanently faithful to his wife. He learned how to be more careful and less impulsive in his frequent meetings with Heather.

Alex, Jasmine, and Heather seem caught in the eternal triangle, and it's not too hard to see how it happened. When Alex and Jasmine married, the balances in their Love Bank accounts stood at the usual all-time highs. But as expectations weren't fulfilled and needs weren't met, Alex became vulnerable to someone else who met his important emotional needs. After that first lunch, Heather's account in Alex's Love Bank mounted rapidly. The affair developed and Alex wound up in love with her. He felt trapped; he couldn't seem to do without either woman. Jasmine was the mother of his children and he knew that they needed their mom and dad to stay together. He had also made a commitment to her, that they would be married for life. But he was in love with Heather.

Steps to Surviving an Affair

Often people ask, "How do you help people like Alex and Jasmine survive an affair? What do you tell a couple when this actually happens to them?"

Frankly, when I first started counseling couples caught in the snare of infidelity, I didn't think that their marriages could survive. At best, I thought they might stick it out for the sake of their children in a lifetime of resentment and regret. I had no idea that they could survive the ordeal to create a better marriage than they had ever experienced.

As it turns out, I've discovered that really the only way to survive an affair is for a couple to turn their marriage into a passionate and fulfilling experience. Unless they have a better marriage than ever before, spouses don't stay together.

My plan to achieve this remarkable result takes a couple down a very narrow path. There are plenty of rules to follow, and without the complete cooperation of both spouses, it won't work. But when the plan is followed, the results are outstanding, and there are thousands of happy couples who bear witness to its amazing rate of success.

Step 1: End the Affair

The first step on the path to surviving an affair is for it to end. An affair ends when the straying spouse ceases all contact with his or her lover and never sees or talks to that person again. Time and again I've watched what happens when a drastic and decisive break with a lover is not made. They try to remain "friends" and maintain casual social contact. But inevitably they find their way back to each other's arms. It seems that when it comes to this one person, the spouse exhibits incredibly flawed judgment and almost irresistible force draws him or her back.

But even if there were no risk of rekindling an affair, if any contact continues, the affair still remains alive in the mind of the betrayed spouse. Since an affair is the most hurtful and selfish act that one spouse can inflict on the other, any contact restores the memory and perpetuates the pain. Wives have told me that their husband's affair was worse than being raped. Men have said their wife's affair was worse than losing a child. It's the ultimate betrayal.

For some, the affair ends the right way. The unfaithful spouse sends a letter to the lover that communicates how much suffering the affair caused the betrayed spouse and how thoughtless it was; the letter expresses a desire to rebuild the marriage and makes it clear that all contact must be terminated forever. The betrayed spouse reads the letter and approves of it before it's sent. After the letter is sent, extraordinary precautions that I'll explain in the next step are taken to avoid future contact with the lover.

But most affairs end the wrong way—they die a natural death. Instead of taking control of the situation and making a decision to end it, most unfaithful spouses continue in the relationship as long as possible. Affairs, however, don't usually last very long. I estimate that 95 percent of them don't last two years. The few couples who eventually marry have an extremely fragile relationship and are much more likely to divorce than the average couple. So if an affair doesn't end the right way, it will almost always end, even if it's the wrong way.

If your unfaithful spouse is unwilling to end an affair the right way, I know of a way to help speed up its demise: expose it. Your family should know—your parents, your siblings, and even your children. The family of your spouse's lover should also know, especially the lover's spouse. The pastor of your church should be informed as well. Exposure of an affair is like opening a moldy closet to the light of day. Affairs do well when they're conducted in secret, but when they're in full view for all to see, they appear as they are—incredibly foolish and thoughtless.

Even if exposure were to be ineffective in ending an affair, I'd recommend it anyway. The betrayed spouse needs as much support as possible, and exposure helps friends and relatives understand what's going on. Keeping an affair secret is no real help to anyone, and I've been amazed at how well exposing it dismantles the illusion that an affair rests on. Instead of assuming that the relationship is made in heaven, an unfaithful spouse quickly senses that it's a one-way ticket to hell on earth.

The first reaction of an unfaithful spouse to exposure is to try to turn the tables on the betrayed spouse. "I will never be able to forgive you for hurting me this way. Don't you ever think about how I'd be affected by this?" Of course, it's really the affair that hurts. The exposure simply identifies the source of the pain. The unfaithful spouse should be the one begging for forgiveness.

In spite of the suffering that an affair inflicts on a betrayed spouse, during this period of exposure, he or she should try to make as many Love Bank deposits and as few withdrawals as possible. If you argue about the affair, you'll damage recovery. Insist on the unfaithful spouse's complete separation from the lover (no contact for life) but don't fight about it. I call this strategy to end the affair Plan A.

If exposure doesn't end the affair immediately, my advice regarding what to do next is different for husbands and wives. I encourage most husbands to try to stick to avoiding arguments and to meet their unfaithful wife's basic needs (Plan A) as long as possible (six months to a year). But I encourage most wives to separate after about three weeks if their husband is still in contact with his lover. My experience has taught me that the health of most women deteriorates quickly and significantly while living with an unfaithful husband. Men, on the other hand, tend to be able to weather the storm longer with fewer emotional or physical effects. I call the strategy of a complete separation Plan B.

In addition to avoiding health problems, a separation also helps keep the unfaithful spouse's account in the betrayed spouse's Love Bank from dwindling any further. Daily interaction with an unfaithful spouse causes such large withdrawals that a separation with no contact between spouses can actually help the marriage by temporarily freezing the betrayed spouse's Love Bank. When the affair is over, the betrayed spouse is less likely to divorce when the unfaithful spouse wants to give the marriage a chance to recover.

Yet another advantage to separation is that some of the basic needs met by the betrayed spouse suddenly disappear. This is especially true when a couple has children. Often an unfaithful spouse overlooks the betrayed spouse's contribution to the family. While the lover may meet two basic needs that were unmet by the betrayed spouse, the betrayed spouse may have been meeting the other three that cannot be easily met by the lover. During a separation, the unfaithful spouse can become acutely aware of what he or she is missing.

When a betrayed spouse decides that it's time to separate, I recommend complete separation with absolutely no direct contact (Plan B). The unfaithful spouse should be given the choice of having contact with the betrayed spouse or the lover, but not both. Someone should be appointed to go between spouses, delivering messages and children during visitation. But until the unfaithful spouse promises to completely end the affair, with absolutely no contact with the lover, the separation should continue. After the separation has lasted two years, with the unfaithful spouse's contact with the lover continuing, I generally recommend a divorce.

Step 2: Create Transparency

When a wayward spouse ends the affair and agrees to rebuild the marriage, extraordinary precautions must be taken to guarantee that there will be no relapses. Affairs thrive on what I've called a *secret second life*. It's what you do under the radar. You know, or at least suspect, that your spouse wouldn't approve, so a part of your life is hidden from him or her. When a spouse is able to come and go without any accountability, he or she, like Alex, can have an affair with relative impunity. The temptation of an affair is great because there's little to stop it.

So I encourage couples to end their secret second life by being *transparent* in the way they live their lives. This not only guards against affairs but also helps create intimacy and build compatibility. It's not a punishment for bad behavior—it's an essential ingredient for a healthy marriage.

Transparency occurs when couples follow the Policy of Radical Honesty that I introduced to you in chapter 7: *Reveal to your spouse as much information about yourself as you know—your thoughts, feelings, habits, likes, dislikes, past history, daily activities, and future plans.*

Nothing should be hidden. Passwords, email, text messages, telephone logs, computer histories, and all other forms of communication are made readily available to a spouse. It's the way my wife, Joyce, and I have lived during our forty-eight years of marriage. By revealing everything we know about ourselves, we have avoided an affair, and our transparency has helped our marriage in a host of other ways too. It's not a lifetime prison sentence, where disclosure prevents us from having what we need most—it's the formula for a very fulfilling life.

If I were to counsel Alex, I would encourage him to give Jasmine a twenty-four-hour-a-day schedule of his whereabouts, and Jasmine should do the same. Such a schedule is essential in a great marriage because spouses who are partners in life check with each other throughout the day to coordinate their decisions and activities. Jasmine should call him several times a day, and he should call her as well, just so they can check in with each other.

How does this twenty-four-hour-a-day checking feel? Admittedly, there is one real drawback in arranging for this kind of checkup system for someone like Alex. While it will provide Jasmine some reassurance, it is likely to be very annoying to Alex, at least at the beginning. Being accustomed to an independent lifestyle, he must now account for his time and activities. He must consider Jasmine's feelings whenever he does anything. That's what couples do in successful marriages, but Alex hasn't learned to be thoughtful when he makes decisions and, at first, he will feel as if he's married to a parole officer.

Typically, a straying spouse, confronted with the demands of transparency and having no contact with his former lover, responds with total depression. Alex may be trying to save his marriage but he feels miserable. Now cut off from Heather—somebody he loves very much and who met some of his most important emotional needs—and with the checkup going, he feels trapped.

Step 3: Meet Each Other's Basic Needs

When the decision is finally made to reconcile and to avoid all contact with the lover, it's usually with the hope that the spouse can learn to meet needs met by the lover much more easily than the lover can meet needs met by the spouse. This is certainly true when the couple has children. The lover will simply never be able to take the place of the spouse in the family, but the spouse *can* take the place of the lover.

My primary goal in helping couples recover after an affair is for them to establish a romantic relationship that's just as passionate as the affair. I don't want their choice to be between passion and reason—the affair offering passion and the marriage offering reason. I want them to have passion *and* reason, something that can be found only in their marriage.

If all goes according to my plan, Jasmine will make herself available to Alex sexually and start joining him in some of his favorite activities. An ideal scenario would find her reading a book about computers and programming to understand better what he does for a living, and to put icing on the cake, she could start giving him more support at home and stop criticizing him about how he doesn't earn enough money or do enough around the house.

All this could take many weeks or months. Probably Alex didn't show Jasmine enough affection, and that's why she resisted him sexually. In addition, Alex needs some coaching in having conversations with Jasmine that will be enjoyable for her. Instead of simply judging Jasmine for not being interested in his computer world, he will have to learn how to talk to her about *her* interests and feelings. Jasmine needs very deeply the quality of conversation Alex shared with Heather.

Obviously Jasmine's basic need for honesty and openness has fallen into serious disrepair. Alex will have to work hard and long to regain her trust, but he can do it if he learns how to become transparent with her.

If I counseled Alex and Jasmine, I would make a special point to warn Jasmine that she has started down a long and bumpy road. In fact, for a while, she may receive little positive return for her efforts. Jasmine should not expect that, as a result of all the changes in her behavior, Alex will suddenly become more loving, caring, and faithful. Rather, as I mentioned, Alex will react initially with depression. If he describes his thoughts honestly, he will tell Jasmine he spends a great deal of time thinking about Heather. Jasmine could even expect some lying and deceit on Alex's part at first. Alex will feel tempted to try to sneak away to meet Heather again.

Regardless of how well Jasmine meets Alex's needs, he will remain in love with Heather for some time to come. Even if the spouses reignite the flame of their own love by meeting each other's five basic needs, all their efforts may not completely extinguish the flame of love ignited by Alex's affair with Heather. It may burn low but never go out completely. Just as an alcoholic remains addicted to alcohol the rest of his life and never dares to touch another drink, Alex will remain vulnerable to Heather for life and should not ever see her again.

Usually I've found that breaking a man away from his lover after he reconciles with his wife proves more difficult than breaking a woman away from her lover. I am not sure why this is so. Perhaps women feel more uncomfortable loving two men, while men adjust better to multiple relationships. Throughout history, in the common system of polygamy, men have supported many women, but most societies have not permitted women to do the same. Sociologists have assumed this discrimination had an economic base (men could support women, but women could not usually support men), but the reason may also turn out to be emotional—men usually enjoy having several wives, while most women find having several husbands repulsive.

A Stronger Marriage

A person who discovers his or her spouse in an affair experiences one of the most severe blows anyone could possibly sustain. It also sends both partners on an emotional roller coaster. But when a couple follow my narrow path to recovery, they often tell me that they have built a better love relationship than they ever would have had if the affair had not jolted them into constructive action. The affair provides the traumatic trigger that finally gets the couple to meet each other's basic needs. Once they start meeting those basic needs, their marriage becomes what it was supposed to have been all along.

Granted, it's certainly more difficult to learn to meet each other's basic needs after an affair than it would have been before an affair. And it's a lot more painful. But with or without an affair, couples can create a very passionate and fulfilling marriage if they simply learn to meet each other's basic needs.

Most people who have never been through recovery after an affair feel that they could never love or trust an unfaithful spouse again. But the thousands of couples whom I've guided down this narrow path are living proof that this is not true.

From Incompatible to Irresistible

14

Before I finish this book, I want to draw your attention to two important words: *incompatible* and *irresistible*. Within the definitions of these words lies the key to understanding and applying to your own marriage the insights I have presented. According to *The American Heritage Dictionary*, the definition of *incompatible* is "inharmonious; antagonistic." The definition of *irresistible* is "having an overpowering appeal."

When a husband and wife can't get along, we may describe them as *incompatible*. Yet at one time, we would have called those same two people *irresistible* to each other. Because they found each other irresistible, they made a lifetime commitment in marriage. Couples start out irresistible and only become incompatible as they leave each other's basic needs unmet. When someone outside the marriage offers to meet those needs, an affair starts. Then the lover becomes irresistible.

But saying the lover is irresistible can be misleading. The lover is seldom *totally* irresistible. In most affairs he or she meets only some—usually one or two—of the basic needs of the straying spouse. The betrayed spouse still fulfills the other three or four basic needs. As I've tried to show time and again, when the straying spouse is caught in the web of an affair, he or she feels a strong need for both people—the spouse left at home and the lover. The thought of losing either of them seems unbearable.

Some people I counsel manage to bite the bullet and make a choice between the two. Some choose the spouse, and some choose the lover. In either case they move from guilt and shame to grief and pain. They feel and act depressed because the needs once met by the person they chose to leave now go unmet.

For example, when a straying husband chooses to return to his wife, he probably feels that he has made some great sacrifice for his family. In most cases he has been forced to give up a satisfying sexual relationship—perhaps the first he has ever known in his life. Any good feelings he may derive from "having done the right thing" do little to lessen his pain or cool his resentment at the loss of what he had in the affair.

If this same straying man chooses his lover, he feels nearly overwhelmed by guilt and shame for having abandoned a wife who has loved and cared for him in many ways. If children are involved, the guilt and shame multiply rapidly. A common lie spread on TV talk shows and in popular books and articles is that divorce doesn't necessarily damage children. Granted, in some exceptional cases, a divorce may be the better of two evils—for example, when a marriage involves severe alcoholism, child (and wife) abuse, insanity, and so on. But in the vast majority of cases I've witnessed, divorce devastates children. To rationalize otherwise is not only stupid, it is cruel.

In my experience, the spouse trapped in an affair comes through the experience relatively healthy when he or she chooses to resolve incompatibility at home and rebuild the marriage. But those I have counseled who have abandoned their marriage in favor of the affair suffer relentless guilt. Those few who manage to avoid the natural death of most affairs and marry their lover find the same problems cropping up in their new marriage. If they ever resolve these problems, they usually know they could have done the same thing to save their first marriage.

The Cure for Incompatibility

The quickest cure for incompatibility and the fastest road to becoming irresistible lie in meeting each other's most important emotional needs.

Happily married couples are already aware of this principle and have learned how to make their marriage a full-time priority. These couples invest the *effort* and they put it in the *right places*.

I have seen this principle work in many different situations. For example, I once managed a dating service in the Twin Cities area. A dating service is designed to help people with common interests and objectives meet each other. But soon after I opened the service, I began to see a very real problem. Those who had enrolled—some five hundred—needed more than just an opportunity to meet each other. Almost without exception these people lacked skills in meeting the emotional needs of others. Yet each of them eagerly sought someone else who would be highly skilled in meeting *their* needs and who would take care of them. They complained that they met only selfish and insensitive people. Of course they could not see their own selfishness and insensitivity.

So I reorganized the dating service. Rather than help my subscribers meet eligible people, I helped them become eligible people to meet, developing skills and other qualities that would make them attractive to the opposite sex.

A number of the dating-service subscribers bought in to my new concept and took the pains necessary to become skillful in meeting the needs of other people. For these men and women, my dating service was a roaring success, and they no longer needed a dating service to introduce them to anyone. Their newly acquired abilities made them attractive to the opposite sex wherever they went. Many of them married within two years.

I believe our society's failure to train people in meeting the needs of others—especially the needs of a marriage partner—has played a large part in our high divorce rate. Marriage is not a simple social institution that everyone enters into because eventually he or she "falls in love and lives happily ever after." As long as we fail to see marriage as a complex relationship that requires special training and abilities to meet the needs of a member of the opposite sex, we will continue to see a discouraging and devastating divorce rate.

At a very young age, children should be trained to meet the needs and expectations that will be laid on them if and when they enter marriage. There is no reason we must see so many marriages that barely hold together or that drift into affairs.

Much of this book deals with what people call "bad" marriages—those that wind up in affairs and divorce. I have tried to give advice on how to avoid an affair or survive one. But in truth you can also use this advice to take an acceptable or even a good marriage and make it into an absolutely outstanding relationship in which each partner is irresistible to the other. Fortunately, you need not merely dream about becoming irresistible, hoping that it happens if and when you find just the right shampoo, deodorant, or perfume. You can really be irresistible.

Before I do a quick review of what it takes to be an irresistible man or woman, let me repeat what I wrote in the first chapter of this book: "Every person is unique. While men *on the average* pick a particular five emotional needs as their most important and women *on the average* pick another five, *any individual* can and does pick any combination of the basic ten. So although I have identified the most important emotional needs of the average man and woman, I don't know the emotional needs of any particular husband and wife. And since I'm in the business of saving individual marriages, not average marriages, you should identify the combinations of needs that are unique to your marriage."

So this review of what it takes, on average, to be an irresistible man or woman should be read with the understanding that you and your spouse will modify it to reflect your unique combination of important emotional needs.

The Irresistible Man

A husband can make himself irresistible to his wife by learning to meet her five most important emotional needs.

1. *Affection.* Her husband tells her that he cares for her with words, cards, flowers, gifts, and common courtesies. He hugs and kisses her many times each day, creating an environment of affection that clearly and repeatedly expresses his care for her.
2. *Conversation.* He sets aside time every day to talk to her. They may talk about events in their lives, their children, their feelings, or their plans. But whatever the topic, she enjoys the conversation because it is never demanding, judgmental, or angry but always informative

and constructive. She talks to him as much as she would like, and he responds with interest. He is never too busy "to just talk."

3. *Honesty and openness.* He tells her everything about himself, leaving nothing out that might later surprise her. He describes his positive and negative feelings, events of his past, his daily schedule, and his plans for the future. He never leaves her with a false impression and is truthful about his thoughts, feelings, intentions, and behavior.

4. *Financial support.* He assumes the responsibility to house, feed, and clothe the family. If his income is insufficient to provide essential support, he resolves the problem by upgrading his skills to increase his salary. He does not work long hours, keeping himself from his wife and family, but is able to provide necessary support by working a forty- to fifty-hour week. While he encourages his wife to pursue a career if it is her desire, he does not depend on her salary for family living expenses.

5. *Family commitment.* He commits sufficient time and energy to the moral and educational development of the children. He reads to them, engages in sports with them, and takes them on frequent outings. He reads books and attends lectures with his wife on the subject of child development so they will do a good job training the children. They discuss training methods and objectives until they agree. He does not proceed with any plan of training discipline without her approval and recognizes that his care of the children is critically important to her.

When a woman finds a man who exhibits all five qualities, she will find him irresistible.

The Irresistible Woman

A wife makes herself irresistible to her husband by learning to meet his five most important emotional needs.

1. *Sexual fulfillment.* His wife meets this need by becoming a terrific sexual partner. She studies her own sexual response to recognize

and understand what brings out the best in her; then she shares this information with him, and together they learn to have a sexual relationship that both find repeatedly satisfying and enjoyable.

2. *Recreational companionship.* She develops an interest in the recreational activities he likes most and tries to become proficient at them. If she finds she cannot enjoy them, she encourages him to consider other activities that they can do together. She becomes his favorite recreational companion, and he associates her with his most enjoyable moments of relaxation.

3. *Physical attractiveness.* She keeps herself physically fit with diet and exercise and she wears her hair, makeup, and clothes in a way that he finds attractive and tasteful. He is attracted to her in private and proud of her in public.

4. *Domestic support.* She creates a home that offers him a refuge from the stresses of life. She manages the household responsibilities in a way that encourages him to spend time at home enjoying his family.

5. *Admiration.* She understands and appreciates him more than anyone else. She reminds him of his value and achievements and helps him maintain self-confidence. She avoids criticizing him. She is proud of him, not out of duty, but from a profound respect for the man she has come to know better than anyone else.

When a man finds a woman who exhibits all five qualities, he will find her irresistible.

Discover Your Most Important Emotional Needs

You may still be unsure that the emotional needs I've described are *your* most important needs—or the most important needs of your spouse. As I said, I cannot say for certain which of these needs apply to you or your spouse, so I've provided an opportunity for you and your spouse to find out for yourselves.

In appendix A, I have written a short description of each of the ten emotional needs. Then, in appendix B, there is an Emotional Needs Questionnaire for you to complete. The questionnaire will help you determine which of the ten emotional needs are most important to you and your spouse.

Make two copies—one for you and one for your spouse—of the Emotional Needs Questionnaire. Make enlarged copies, so you will have space to write your answers. Before you complete them, be sure to read appendix A to become familiar with all ten emotional needs.

On the last page of the Emotional Needs Questionnaire, you have an opportunity to rank all ten needs in order of their importance to you. This final ranking helps your spouse put your emotional needs in perspective. He or she will know where to put the greatest effort to fulfill your happiness if you rank the needs honestly.

Avoid the temptation of putting only *unfulfilled* needs at the top of the list. Some of your most important needs may already be met. Don't use the list simply to get your spouse's attention; use it to accurately describe your needs. Remember, the needs at the top of the list should be those that give you the greatest pleasure when met and frustrate you the most when unmet.

I have been saying all along in this book that, while both men and women share most of the ten basic needs, the order of their priorities is usually opposite. The top five needs for men are usually the bottom five for women, and the top five for women are usually the bottom five for men. When you indicate clearly the priority of your needs to your spouse, he or she can invest energy and attention where it does you the most good.

Few experiences compare with falling in love, but many couples fail to realize that love needs constant nurture and care. I've tried to give you some guidelines for providing that care and for building a marriage that sustains the feeling of love. If you've lost that feeling, and must learn new skills to meet each other's emotional needs more effectively, it may be hard work at first. But after you've learned to be an expert husband and wife, your care for each other will become almost effortless. Take it from a man who's been in love for the entire forty-eight years of my marriage—it's a lot less work to have a sensational marriage than it is to have a horrible marriage. When you've learned how to meet each other's most important emotional needs, you will have mastered one of life's most valuable lessons.

Both you and your spouse should complete your copies of the questionnaire to help you both communicate your needs and how you've done in meeting them. With the increased understanding that comes through this communication, I hope you will build a long, passionate, and successful marriage.

Appendix A

The Most Important Emotional Needs

Before you complete the Emotional Needs Questionnaire in appendix B, review the following ten most important emotional needs.

Affection

Quite simply, affection is the expression of care. It symbolizes security, protection, comfort, and approval—vitally important ingredients in any relationship. When one spouse is affectionate to the other, the following messages are sent:

1. You are important to me, and I will care for you and protect you.
2. I'm concerned about the problems you face and will be there for you when you need me.

A hug can say these things. When we hug our friends and relatives, we are demonstrating our care for them. And there are other ways to show our affection—a greeting card, an "I love you" note, a bouquet of flowers, holding hands, walks after dinner, back rubs, phone calls, and conversations with thoughtful and loving expressions can all communicate affection.

Sex and affection are often confused, especially by men. Affection is an expression of care that is nonsexual and can be appropriately given to friends, relatives, children, and even pets. However, affectionate expressions, such as hugging and kissing, that are done with a sexual motive are actually sex, not affection.

Affection is, for many, the essential cement of a relationship. Without it, people can feel totally alienated. With it, they become emotionally bonded. If you feel terrific when your spouse is affectionate and you feel terrible when there is not enough affection, you have the emotional need for affection.

Sexual Fulfillment

Most people know whether they have a need for sex, but if you have any uncertainty, I will point out some of the most obvious symptoms.

Usually a sexual need predates your current relationship and is somewhat independent of your relationship. While you may have discovered a deep desire to make love to your spouse since you've been in love, it isn't quite the same thing as a sexual need. Wanting to make love when you are in love is sometimes merely a reflection of wanting to be emotionally and physically close.

Sexual fantasies are a dead giveaway for a sexual need. In general, fantasies are good indicators of emotional needs, with your most common fantasies reflecting your most important needs. If you have imagined what it would be like having your sexual need met in the most fulfilling ways, you probably have a sexual need. The more the fantasy is employed, the greater your need. And the way your sexual need is met in your fantasy can be a good indicator of your sexual predispositions and orientation.

When you married, you and your spouse both promised to be faithful to each other for life. This means that you agreed to be each other's only sexual partner "until death do us part." You made this commitment because you trusted each other to meet your sexual needs, to be sexually available and responsive. The need for sex, then, is a very exclusive need, and if you have it, you will be very dependent on your spouse to meet it for you. You have no other ethical choice.

Intimate Conversation

Intimate conversation is different from ordinary conversation. Its content focuses attention on very personal interests, problems, topics, and events. It's intimate because you would generally not reveal such personal information to just anyone. Only those who seem to care about you and would be willing to help you think through the problems you face are worthy of intimate conversation. If you have this need, whoever meets it best may deposit so many love units that you fall in love with that person. So if it's your need, be sure that your spouse is the one who meets it the best and most often.

Men and women don't have too much difficulty talking to each other during courtship. That's a time of information gathering for both partners. Both are highly motivated to discover each other's likes and dislikes, personal background, current interests, and plans for the future. They are also willing to demonstrate their care for each other by trying to help solve problems that are raised.

But after marriage, many women find that the man who would spend hours talking to them on the telephone now seems to have lost all interest in talking to them and spends his spare time watching television or reading. Since the woman's need for intimate conversation was fulfilled during courtship, she expects it to be met after marriage.

If you see conversation as a practical necessity, primarily as a means to an end, you probably don't have much of a need for it. But if you have a craving just to talk to someone about what's going on in your life, if you pick up the telephone just because you feel like talking, if you enjoy conversation in its own right, consider intimate conversation to be one of your most important emotional needs.

Recreational Companionship

A need for recreational companionship combines two needs into one: the need to engage in recreational activities and the need to have a companion.

During your courtship, you and your spouse were probably each other's favorite recreational companions. It's not uncommon for women to join men in hunting, fishing, watching football, or other activities they would never choose on their own. They simply want to spend as much time as possible with the man they like, and that means going where he goes.

The same is true of men. Shopping centers are not unfamiliar to men in love. They will also take their dates out to dinner, watch romantic movies, and attend concerts and plays. They take every opportunity to be with someone they like and try to enjoy the activity to guarantee more dates in the future.

I won't deny that marriage changes a relationship considerably. But does it have to end the activities that helped make the relationship so compatible? Can't a husband's favorite recreational companion be his wife and vice versa?

If recreational activities are important to you and you like to have someone join you in them to be fulfilling, include recreational companionship on your list of needs. Think about it for a moment in terms of the Love Bank. How much do you enjoy these activities and how many love units would your spouse be depositing whenever you enjoyed them together? What a waste it would be if all those love units were deposited into someone else's Love Bank account! And if it would be someone of the opposite sex, it would be downright dangerous.

Who should get credit for all the love units that are created when you are enjoying yourself recreationally? It's the one you should love the most, your spouse. That's precisely why I encourage a husband and wife to be each other's favorite recreational companion. It's one of the simplest ways to deposit love units.

Honesty and Openness

Most of us want an honest relationship with our spouse. But some of us have a need for such a relationship because honesty and openness give us a sense of security.

To feel secure, we want accurate information about our spouse's thoughts, feelings, habits, likes, dislikes, personal history, daily activities, and plans for the future. If a spouse does not provide honest and open communication, trust can be undermined and the feelings of security can eventually be destroyed. Then the partner can't trust the signals that are being sent and has no foundation on which to build a solid relationship. Instead of adjusting to each other, the couple feel off balance; instead of growing together, they grow apart.

Aside from the practical considerations of honesty and openness, there are some of us who feel happy and fulfilled when our spouse reveals his or her most private thoughts to us. And we feel very frustrated when they are hidden. That reaction is evidence of an emotional need, one that can and should be met in marriage.

Physical Attractiveness

For many people, physical appearance can become one of the greatest sources of love units. If you have this need, an attractive person will not only get your attention, but may distract you from whatever you're doing. In fact that's what may have first drawn you to your spouse—his or her physical appearance.

There are some who consider this need to be temporary and important only in the beginning of a relationship. After a couple get to know each other better, some feel that physical attractiveness usually takes a backseat to deeper and more intimate needs. But that's not been my experience, nor has it been the experience of many people I've counseled, particularly men. For many, the need for physical attractiveness continues on throughout marriage, and just seeing the spouse looking attractive deposits love units.

Among the various aspects of physical attractiveness, weight generally gets the most attention. However, choice of clothing, hairstyle, makeup, and personal hygiene also come together to make a person attractive. It can be very subjective, and you are the judge of what is attractive to you.

If the attractiveness of your spouse makes you feel great, and loss of that attractiveness would make you feel very frustrated, you should probably include this category on your list of important emotional needs.

Financial Support

Many people marry for the financial security their spouse provides them. In other words, part of the reason they marry is for money. Is financial support one of your important emotional needs?

If may be difficult for you to know if you have a need for financial support, especially if your spouse has always been gainfully employed. But what if, before marriage, your spouse had told you not to expect any income from him or her? Would it have affected your decision to marry? Or what if your spouse could not find work, and you had to support him or her financially throughout life? Would that withdraw love units?

You may have a need for financial support if you expect your spouse to earn a living. But you definitely have that need if you do not expect to be earning a living yourself, at least during part of your marriage.

What constitutes financial support? Earning enough to buy everything you could possibly desire or earning just enough to get by? Different spouses would answer this differently, and the same spouse might answer differently in different stages of life. But like many of these emotional needs, financial support is sometimes difficult to discuss. As a result, many spouses have hidden expectations, assumptions, and resentments. Try to understand what you expect from your spouse financially to feel fulfilled. And what would it take for you to feel frustrated? Your analysis will help you determine if you have a need for financial support.

Domestic Support

The need for domestic support is a time bomb. At first, it seems irrelevant, a throwback to more primitive times. But for many couples, the need explodes after a few years of marriage, surprising both husband and wife.

In earlier generations, it was assumed that all husbands had this need and all wives would naturally meet it. Times have changed, and needs have changed along with them. Now many of the men I counsel would rather have their wife meet their needs for affection or conversation, needs that have traditionally been more characteristic of women. And many women, especially career women, gain a great deal of pleasure having their husband create a peaceful and well-managed home environment.

Marriage usually begins with a willingness of both spouses to share domestic responsibilities. It's common for newlyweds to wash dishes together, make the bed together, and divide many household tasks. The groom welcomes his wife's help in doing what he had to do by himself as a bachelor. At this point in marriage, neither of them would identify domestic support as an important emotional need. But the time bomb is ticking.

When does the need for domestic support explode? When the children arrive! Children create huge needs—both a greater need for income and greater domestic responsibilities. The previous division of labor becomes obsolete. Both spouses must take on new responsibilities—and which ones will they take?

Domestic support includes cooking meals, washing dishes, washing and ironing clothes, cleaning house, and child care. If you feel very fulfilled when your spouse does these things, or takes charge of getting them done, and very annoyed when they are not done, you have the need for domestic support.

Family Commitment

In addition to a greater need for income and domestic responsibilities, the arrival of children creates in many people the need for family commitment. Again, if you don't have children yet, you may not sense this need, but when the first child arrives, a change may take place that you didn't anticipate.

Family commitment is not child care—feeding, clothing, or watching over children to keep them safe. Child care falls under the category of domestic support. Family commitment, on the other hand, is a responsibility for the development of the children, teaching them the values of cooperation and care for each other. It is spending quality time with your children to help them develop into successful adults.

Evidence of this need is a craving for your spouse's involvement in the educational and moral development of your children. When he or she is helping care for them, you feel very fulfilled, and when he or she neglects their development, you feel very frustrated.

We all want our children to be successful, but if you have the need for family commitment, your spouse's participation in family activities will make large Love Bank deposits. And your spouse's neglect of your children will make noticeable withdrawals.

Admiration

If you have the need for admiration, you may have fallen in love with your spouse partly because of his or her compliments to you. Some people just love to be told that they are appreciated. Your spouse may also have been careful not to criticize you. If you have a need for admiration, the slightest criticism may hurt you deeply.

Many of us have a deep desire to be respected, valued, and appreciated by our spouse. We need to be affirmed clearly and often. There's nothing wrong with feeling this way. Even God wants us to appreciate him!

Appreciation is one of the easiest needs to meet. Just a compliment, and presto, you've made your spouse's day. On the other hand, it's also easy to be critical. A trivial word of rebuke can be very upsetting to some people, ruining their day and withdrawing love units at an alarming rate.

Your spouse may have the power to build up or deplete his or her account in your Love Bank with just a few words. If you can be affected that easily, be sure to add admiration to your list of important emotional needs.

Appendix B

Emotional Needs Questionnaire

© 1986 by Willard F. Harley, Jr.

Name_____ Date_____

This questionnaire is designed to help you determine your most important emotional needs and evaluate your spouse's effectiveness in meeting those needs. Answer all the questions as candidly as possible. Do not try to minimize any needs that you feel have been unmet. If your answers require more space, use and attach a separate sheet of paper.

Your spouse should complete a separate Emotional Needs Questionnaire so that you can discover his or her needs and evaluate your effectiveness in meeting those needs.

When you have completed this questionnaire, go through it a second time to be certain your answers accurately reflect your feelings. Do not erase your original answers, but cross them out lightly so that your spouse can see the corrections and discuss them with you.

The final page of this questionnaire asks you to identify and rank five of the ten needs in order of their importance to you. The most important emotional needs are those that give you the most pleasure when met and frustrate you the most when unmet. Resist the temptation to identify as most important only those needs that your spouse is *not* presently meeting. Include *all* your emotional needs in your consideration of those that are most important.

You have the permission of the publisher to photocopy the questionnaire for use in your own marriage. I recommend that you enlarge it 125 percent so that you'll have plenty of room to write in your responses.

1. **Affection.** Showing care through words, cards, gifts, hugs, kisses, and courtesies; creating an environment that clearly and repeatedly expresses care.

   A. **Need for affection:** Indicate how much you need affection by circling the appropriate number.

   | 0 | 1 | 2 | 3 | 4 | 5 | 6 |

   I have no need
   for affection

   I have a moderate need
   for affection

   I have a great need
   for affection

   If or when your spouse is *not* affectionate with you, how do you feel? (Circle the appropriate letter.)
   a. Very unhappy
   b. Somewhat unhappy
   c. Neither happy nor unhappy
   d. Happy not to be shown affection

   If or when your spouse is affectionate to you, how do you feel? (Circle the appropriate letter.)
   a. Very happy
   b. Somewhat happy
   c. Neither happy nor unhappy
   d. Unhappy to be shown affection

   B. **Evaluation of spouse's affection:** Indicate your satisfaction with your spouse's affection toward you by circling the appropriate number.

   | -3 | -2 | 1 | 0 | 1 | 2 | 3 |

   I am extremely dissatisfied

   I am neither satisfied nor
   dissatisfied

   I am extremely satisfied

   My spouse gives me all the affection I need. ☐ Yes ☐ No

   If your answer is no, how often would you like your spouse to be affectionate with you?

   _____ (write number) times each day/week/month (circle one).

   I like the way my spouse gives me affection. ☐ Yes ☐ No

   If your answer is no, explain how your need for affection could be better satisfied in your marriage._____

   _____

   _____

   _____

2. Sexual fulfillment. A sexual relationship that brings out a predictably enjoyable sexual response in both of you that is frequent enough for both of you.

A. Need for sexual fulfillment: Indicate how much you need sexual fulfillment by circling the appropriate number.

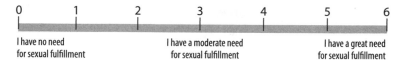

| 0 | 1 | 2 | 3 | 4 | 5 | 6 |

I have no need for sexual fulfillment

I have a moderate need for sexual fulfillment

I have a great need for sexual fulfillment

If or when your spouse *is not* willing to engage in sexual relations with you, how do you feel? (Circle the appropriate letter.)

a. Very unhappy

b. Somewhat unhappy

c. Neither happy nor unhappy

d. Happy not to engage in sexual relations

If or when your spouse engages in sexual relations with you, how do you feel? (Circle the appropriate letter.)

a. Very happy

b. Somewhat happy

c. Neither happy nor unhappy

d. Unhappy to engage in sexual relations

B. Evaluation of sexual relations with your spouse: Indicate your satisfaction with your spouse's sexual relations with you by circling the appropriate number.

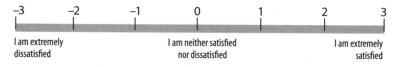

| −3 | −2 | −1 | 0 | 1 | 2 | 3 |

I am extremely dissatisfied

I am neither satisfied nor dissatisfied

I am extremely satisfied

My spouse has sexual relations with me as often as I need. ☐ Yes ☐ No

If your answer is no, how often would you like your spouse to have sex with you?

_____ (write number) times each day/week/month (circle one).

I like the way my spouse has sexual relations with me. ☐ Yes ☐ No

If your answer is no, explain how your need for sexual fulfillment could be better satisfied in your marriage. _____

_____

_____

215

3. **Intimate Conversation.** Talking about events of the day, feelings, and plans; avoiding angry or judgmental statements or dwelling on past mistakes; showing interest in your favorite topics of conversation; balancing conversation; using it to inform, investigate, and understand you; and giving you undivided attention.

A. **Need for intimate conversation:** Indicate how much you need intimate conversation by circling the appropriate number.

| 0 | 1 | 2 | 3 | 4 | 5 | 6 |

I have no need
for intimate conversation

I have a moderate need
for intimate conversation

I have a great need
for intimate conversation

If or when your spouse *is not* willing to talk with you, how do you feel? (Circle the appropriate letter.)

a. Very unhappy
b. Somewhat unhappy

c. Neither happy nor unhappy
d. Happy not to talk

If or when your spouse talks to you, how do you feel? (Circle the appropriate letter.)

a. Very happy
b. Somewhat happy

c. Neither happy nor unhappy
d. Unhappy to talk

B. **Evaluation of intimate conversation with your spouse:** Indicate your satisfaction with your spouse's intimate conversation with you by circling the appropriate number.

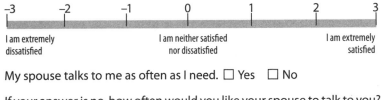

| –3 | –2 | –1 | 0 | 1 | 2 | 3 |

I am extremely
dissatisfied

I am neither satisfied
nor dissatisfied

I am extremely
satisfied

My spouse talks to me as often as I need. ☐ Yes ☐ No

If your answer is no, how often would you like your spouse to talk to you?

_____ (write number) times each day/week/month (circle one).

_____ (write number) hours each day/week/month (circle one).

I like the way my spouse talks to me. ☐ Yes ☐ No

If your answer is no, explain how your need for intimate conversation could be better satisfied in your marriage. _____

_____

4. **Recreational companionship.** Developing interest in your favorite recreational activities, learning to be proficient in them, and joining you in those activities. If any prove to be unpleasant to your spouse after an effort has been made, negotiating new recreational activities that are mutually enjoyable.

   A. **Need for recreational companionship:** Indicate how much you need recreational companionship by circling the appropriate number.

0	1	2	3	4	5	6
I have no need for recreational companionship			I have a moderate need for recreational companionship			I have a great need for recreational companionship

   If or when your spouse *is not* willing to join you in recreational activities, how do you feel? (Circle the appropriate letter.)
   a. Very unhappy
   b. Somewhat unhappy
   c. Neither happy nor unhappy
   d. Happy not to include my spouse

   If or when your spouse joins you in recreational activities, how do you feel? (Circle the appropriate letter.)
   a. Very happy
   b. Somewhat happy
   c. Neither happy nor unhappy
   d. Unhappy to include my spouse

   B. **Evaluation of recreational companionship with your spouse:** Indicate your satisfaction with your spouse's recreational companionship by circling the appropriate number.

-3	-2	-1	0	1	2	3
I am extremely dissatisfied			I am neither satisfied nor dissatisfied			I am extremely satisfied

   My spouse joins me in recreational activities as often as I need.
   ☐ Yes   ☐ No

   If your answer is no, how often would you like your spouse to join you in recreational activities?

   _____ (write number) times each day/week/month (circle one).

   _____ (write number) hours each day/week/month (circle one).

   I like the way my spouse joins me in recreational activities. ☐ Yes   ☐ No

   If your answer is no, explain how your need for recreational companionship could be better satisfied in your marriage. _____

   _____

5. **Honesty and openness.** Revealing positive and negative feelings, events of the past, daily events and schedule, plans for the future; not leaving you with a false impression; answering your questions truthfully.

A. **Need for honesty and openness:** Indicate how much you need honesty and openness by circling the appropriate number.

If or when your spouse *is not* open and honest with you, how do you feel? (Circle the appropriate letter.)
a. Very unhappy   c. Neither happy nor unhappy
b. Somewhat unhappy   d. Happy that my spouse isn't honest and open

If or when your spouse is open and honest with you, how do you feel? (Circle the appropriate letter.)
a. Very happy   c. Neither happy nor unhappy
b. Somewhat happy   d. Unhappy that my spouse is honest and open

B. **Evaluation of spouse's honesty and openness:** Indicate your satisfaction with your spouse's honesty and openness by circling the appropriate number.

In which of the following areas of honesty and openness would you like to see improvement from your spouse? (Circle the letters that apply to you.)
a. Sharing positive and negative emotional reactions to significant aspects of life
b. Sharing information regarding his/her personal history
c. Sharing information about his/her daily activities
d. Sharing information about his/her future schedule and plans

If you circled any of the above, explain how your need for honesty and openness could be better satisfied in your marriage. _____

_____

6. **Physical attractiveness.** Keeping physically fit with diet and exercise; wearing hair, clothing, and (if female) makeup in a way that you find attractive and tasteful.

A. **Need for physical attractiveness:** Indicate how much you need physical attractiveness by circling the appropriate number.

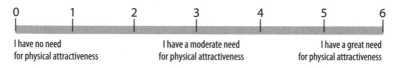

| 0 | 1 | 2 | 3 | 4 | 5 | 6 |

I have no need
for physical attractiveness

I have a moderate need
for physical attractiveness

I have a great need
for physical attractiveness

If or when your spouse *is not* willing to make the most of his or her physical attractiveness, how do you feel? (Circle the appropriate letter.)
a. Very unhappy
b. Somewhat unhappy
c. Neither happy nor unhappy
d. Happy he or she does not make an effort

When your spouse makes the most of his or her physical attractiveness, how do you feel? (Circle the appropriate letter.)
a. Very happy
b. Somewhat happy
c. Neither happy nor unhappy
d. Unhappy to see that he or she makes an effort

B. **Evaluation of spouse's attractiveness:** Indicate your satisfaction with your spouse's attractiveness by circling the appropriate number.

| -3 | -2 | -1 | 0 | 1 | 2 | 3 |

I am extremely
dissatisfied

I am neither satisfied
nor dissatisfied

I am extremely
satisfied

In which of the following characteristics of attractiveness would you like to see improvement from your spouse? (Circle the letters that apply.)
a. Physical fitness and normal weight
b. Attractive choice of clothes
c. Attractive hairstyle
d. Good physical hygiene
e. Attractive facial makeup
f. Other _____

If you circled any of the above, explain how your need for physical attractiveness could be better satisfied in your marriage. _____

_____

_____

_____

7. **Financial support.** Provision of the financial resources to house, feed, and clothe your family at a standard of living acceptable to you, but avoiding travel and working hours that are unacceptable to you.

A. **Need for financial support:** Indicate how much you need financial support by circling the appropriate number.

| 0 | 1 | 2 | 3 | 4 | 5 | 6 |

I have no need
for financial support

I have a moderate need
for financial support

I have a great need
for financial support

If or when your spouse *is not* willing to support you financially, how do you feel? (Circle the appropriate letter.)

a. Very unhappy   c. Neither happy nor unhappy
b. Somewhat unhappy   d. Happy not to be financially supported

If or when your spouse supports you financially, how do you feel? (Circle the appropriate letter.)

a. Very happy   c. Neither happy nor unhappy
b. Somewhat happy   d. Unhappy to be financially supported

B. **Evaluation of spouse's financial support:** Indicate your satisfaction with your spouse's financial support by circling the appropriate number.

| −3 | −2 | −1 | 0 | 1 | 2 | 3 |

I am extremely
dissatisfied

I am neither satisfied
nor dissatisfied

I am extremely
satisfied

How much money would you like your spouse to earn to support you?

_____

_____

How many hours each week would you like your spouse to work? _____

If your spouse is not earning as much as you would like, is not working the hours you would like, does not budget the way you would like, or does not earn an income the way you would like, explain how your need for financial support could be better satisfied in your marriage.

_____

_____

8. **Domestic support.** Creation of a home environment for you that offers a refuge from the stresses of life; managing the home and care of the children—if any are at home—including but not limited to cooking meals, washing dishes, washing and ironing clothes, and housecleaning.

A. **Need for domestic support:** Indicate how much you need domestic support by circling the appropriate number.

0	1	2	3	4	5	6

I have no need
for domestic support

I have a moderate need
for domestic support

I have a great need
for domestic support

If your spouse *is not* willing to provide you with domestic support, how do you feel? (Circle the appropriate letter.)

a. Very unhappy

b. Somewhat unhappy

c. Neither happy nor unhappy

d. Happy not to have domestic support

If or when your spouse provides you with domestic support, how do you feel? (Circle the appropriate letter.)

a. Very happy

b. Somewhat happy

c. Neither happy nor unhappy

d. Unhappy to have domestic support

B. **Evaluation of spouse's domestic support:** Indicate your satisfaction with your spouse's domestic support by circling the appropriate number.

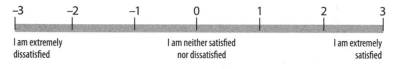

−3	−2	−1	0	1	2	3

I am extremely
dissatisfied

I am neither satisfied
nor dissatisfied

I am extremely
satisfied

My spouse provides me with all the domestic support I need. ☐ Yes ☐ No

I like the way my spouse provides domestic support. ☐ Yes ☐ No

If your answer is no to either of the above questions, explain how your need for domestic support could be better satisfied in your marriage.

_____

_____

_____

_____

_____

9. **Family commitment.** Scheduling sufficient time and energy for the moral and educational development of your children; reading to them, taking them on frequent outings, educating himself or herself in appropriate child-training methods and discussing these methods with you; avoiding any child-training method or disciplinary action that does not have your enthusiastic support.

   A. **Need for family commitment:** Indicate how much you need family commitment by circling the appropriate number.

   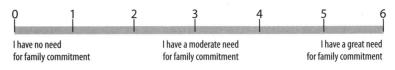

   | 0 | 1 | 2 | 3 | 4 | 5 | 6 |

   I have no need
   for family commitment

   I have a moderate need
   for family commitment

   I have a great need
   for family commitment

   If or when your spouse *is not* willing to provide family commitment, how do you feel? (Circle the appropriate letter.)
   a. Very unhappy
   b. Somewhat unhappy
   c. Neither happy nor unhappy
   d. Happy he or she is not involved

   If or when your spouse provides family commitment, how do you feel? (Circle the appropriate letter.)
   a. Very happy
   b. Somewhat happy
   c. Neither happy nor unhappy
   d. Unhappy he or she is involved in the family

   B. **Evaluation of spouse's family commitment:** Indicate your satisfaction with your spouse's family commitment by circling the appropriate number.

   | −3 | −2 | −1 | 0 | 1 | 2 | 3 |

   I am extremely
   dissatisfied

   I am neither satisfied
   nor dissatisfied

   I am extremely
   satisfied

   My spouse commits enough time to the family. ☐ Yes   ☐ No

   If your answer is no, how often would you like your spouse to join in family activities?

   _____ (write number) times each day/week/month (circle one).

   _____ (write number) hours each day/week/month (circle one).

   I like the way my spouse spends time with the family. ☐ Yes   ☐ No

   If your answer is no, explain how your need for family commitment could be better satisfied in your marriage. _____

   _____

10. **Admiration.** Respecting, valuing, and appreciating you; rarely critical; and expressing admiration to you clearly and often.

   A. **Need for admiration:** Indicate how much you need admiration by circling the appropriate number.

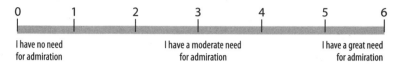

| 0 | 1 | 2 | 3 | 4 | 5 | 6 |

I have no need
for admiration

I have a moderate need
for admiration

I have a great need
for admiration

If or when your spouse *does not* admire you, how do you feel? (Circle the appropriate letter.)

   a. Very unhappy   c. Neither happy nor unhappy

   b. Somewhat unhappy   d. Happy not to be admired

If or when your spouse does admire you, how do you feel? (Circle the appropriate letter.)

   a. Very happy   c. Neither happy nor unhappy

   b. Somewhat happy   d. Unhappy to be admired

   B. **Evaluation of spouse's admiration:** Indicate your satisfaction with your spouse's admiration of you by circling the appropriate number.

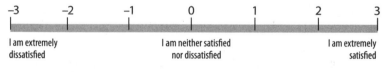

| −3 | −2 | −1 | 0 | 1 | 2 | 3 |

I am extremely
dissatisfied

I am neither satisfied
nor dissatisfied

I am extremely
satisfied

My spouse gives me all the admiration I need. ☐ Yes ☐ No

If your answer is no, how often would you like your spouse to admire you?

_____ (write number) times each day/week/month (circle one).

I like the way my spouse admires me. ☐ Yes ☐ No

If your answer is no, explain how your need for admiration could be better satisfied in your marriage. _____

_____

_____

_____

Ranking Your Emotional Needs

The ten basic emotional needs are listed below. There is also space for you to add other emotional needs that you feel are essential to your marital happiness.

In the space provided before each need, write a number from 1 to 5 that ranks the need's importance to your happiness. Write a 1 before the most important need, a 2 before the next most important, and so on until you have ranked your five most important needs.

To help you rank these needs, imagine that you will have only one need met in your marriage. Which would make you the happiest, knowing that all the others would go unmet? That need should be 1. If only two needs will be met, what would your second selection be? Which five needs, when met, would make you the happiest?

_____ Affection

_____ Sexual fulfillment

_____ Conversation

_____ Recreational companionship

_____ Honesty and openness

_____ Attractiveness of spouse

_____ Financial support

_____ Domestic support

_____ Family commitment

_____ Admiration

_____ _____

_____ _____

Appendix C

Recreational Enjoyment Inventory

Please indicate how much you enjoy, or think you might enjoy, each recreational activity listed below. In the space provided by each activity, under the appropriate column (husband's or wife's), circle one of the numbers to reflect your feelings: 3 = very enjoyable; 2 = enjoyable; 1 = somewhat enjoyable; 0 = no feelings one way or the other; –1 = somewhat unpleasant; –2 = unpleasant; –3 = very unpleasant. Add to the list, in the spaces provided, activities you would enjoy that are not listed. In the third column, add the ratings of both you and your spouse *only if both ratings are positive*. The activities with the highest sum are those that you should select when planning recreational time together.

You have the permission of the publisher to photocopy the questionnaire for use in your own marriage. I recommend that you enlarge it 125 percent so that you'll have plenty of room to write in your responses.

Activity	Husband's Rating	Wife's Rating	Total Rating
Acting	–3 –2 –1 0 1 2 3	–3 –2 –1 0 1 2 3	_____
Aerobic exercise	–3 –2 –1 0 1 2 3	–3 –2 –1 0 1 2 3	_____
Amusement parks	–3 –2 –1 0 1 2 3	–3 –2 –1 0 1 2 3	_____

Activity	Husband's Rating	Wife's Rating	Total Rating
Antique collecting	–3 –2 –1 0 1 2 3	–3 –2 –1 0 1 2 3	_____
Archery	–3 –2 –1 0 1 2 3	–3 –2 –1 0 1 2 3	_____
Astronomy	–3 –2 –1 0 1 2 3	–3 –2 –1 0 1 2 3	_____
Auto customizing	–3 –2 –1 0 1 2 3	–3 –2 –1 0 1 2 3	_____
Auto racing (watching)	–3 –2 –1 0 1 2 3	–3 –2 –1 0 1 2 3	_____
Badminton	–3 –2 –1 0 1 2 3	–3 –2 –1 0 1 2 3	_____
Baseball (watching)	–3 –2 –1 0 1 2 3	–3 –2 –1 0 1 2 3	_____
Baseball (playing)	–3 –2 –1 0 1 2 3	–3 –2 –1 0 1 2 3	_____
Basketball (watching)	–3 –2 –1 0 1 2 3	–3 –2 –1 0 1 2 3	_____
Basketball (playing)	–3 –2 –1 0 1 2 3	–3 –2 –1 0 1 2 3	_____
Bible study	–3 –2 –1 0 1 2 3	–3 –2 –1 0 1 2 3	_____
Bicycling	–3 –2 –1 0 1 2 3	–3 –2 –1 0 1 2 3	_____
Boating	–3 –2 –1 0 1 2 3	–3 –2 –1 0 1 2 3	_____
Bodybuilding	–3 –2 –1 0 1 2 3	–3 –2 –1 0 1 2 3	_____
Bowling	–3 –2 –1 0 1 2 3	–3 –2 –1 0 1 2 3	_____
Boxing (watching)	–3 –2 –1 0 1 2 3	–3 –2 –1 0 1 2 3	_____
Bridge	–3 –2 –1 0 1 2 3	–3 –2 –1 0 1 2 3	_____
Camping	–3 –2 –1 0 1 2 3	–3 –2 –1 0 1 2 3	_____
Canasta	–3 –2 –1 0 1 2 3	–3 –2 –1 0 1 2 3	_____
Canoeing	–3 –2 –1 0 1 2 3	–3 –2 –1 0 1 2 3	_____
Checkers	–3 –2 –1 0 1 2 3	–3 –2 –1 0 1 2 3	_____
Chess	–3 –2 –1 0 1 2 3	–3 –2 –1 0 1 2 3	_____
Church services	–3 –2 –1 0 1 2 3	–3 –2 –1 0 1 2 3	_____
Coin collecting	–3 –2 –1 0 1 2 3	–3 –2 –1 0 1 2 3	_____
Computer programming	–3 –2 –1 0 1 2 3	–3 –2 –1 0 1 2 3	_____
Computer games	–3 –2 –1 0 1 2 3	–3 –2 –1 0 1 2 3	_____
Computer _____	–3 –2 –1 0 1 2 3	–3 –2 –1 0 1 2 3	_____
Concerts (rock music)	–3 –2 –1 0 1 2 3	–3 –2 –1 0 1 2 3	_____
Concerts (classical music)	–3 –2 –1 0 1 2 3	–3 –2 –1 0 1 2 3	_____
Concerts (country music)	–3 –2 –1 0 1 2 3	–3 –2 –1 0 1 2 3	_____
Cribbage	–3 –2 –1 0 1 2 3	–3 –2 –1 0 1 2 3	_____
Croquet	–3 –2 –1 0 1 2 3	–3 –2 –1 0 1 2 3	_____
Dancing (ballroom)	–3 –2 –1 0 1 2 3	–3 –2 –1 0 1 2 3	_____
Dancing (square)	–3 –2 –1 0 1 2 3	–3 –2 –1 0 1 2 3	_____
Dancing (rock)	–3 –2 –1 0 1 2 3	–3 –2 –1 0 1 2 3	_____
Dancing (_____)	–3 –2 –1 0 1 2 3	–3 –2 –1 0 1 2 3	_____

Activity	Husband's Rating	Wife's Rating	Total Rating
Dining out	-3 -2 -1 0 1 2 3	-3 -2 -1 0 1 2 3	_____
Fishing	-3 -2 -1 0 1 2 3	-3 -2 -1 0 1 2 3	_____
Flying (as pilot)	-3 -2 -1 0 1 2 3	-3 -2 -1 0 1 2 3	_____
Flying (as passenger)	-3 -2 -1 0 1 2 3	-3 -2 -1 0 1 2 3	_____
Football (watching)	-3 -2 -1 0 1 2 3	-3 -2 -1 0 1 2 3	_____
Football (playing)	-3 -2 -1 0 1 2 3	-3 -2 -1 0 1 2 3	_____
Gardening	-3 -2 -1 0 1 2 3	-3 -2 -1 0 1 2 3	_____
Genealogical research	-3 -2 -1 0 1 2 3	-3 -2 -1 0 1 2 3	_____
Golf	-3 -2 -1 0 1 2 3	-3 -2 -1 0 1 2 3	_____
Ham radio	-3 -2 -1 0 1 2 3	-3 -2 -1 0 1 2 3	_____
Handball	-3 -2 -1 0 1 2 3	-3 -2 -1 0 1 2 3	_____
Hiking	-3 -2 -1 0 1 2 3	-3 -2 -1 0 1 2 3	_____
Hockey (watching)	-3 -2 -1 0 1 2 3	-3 -2 -1 0 1 2 3	_____
Hockey (playing)	-3 -2 -1 0 1 2 3	-3 -2 -1 0 1 2 3	_____
Horseback riding	-3 -2 -1 0 1 2 3	-3 -2 -1 0 1 2 3	_____
Horse shows (watching)	-3 -2 -1 0 1 2 3	-3 -2 -1 0 1 2 3	_____
Horse racing	-3 -2 -1 0 1 2 3	-3 -2 -1 0 1 2 3	_____
Horseshoe pitching	-3 -2 -1 0 1 2 3	-3 -2 -1 0 1 2 3	_____
Hot air ballooning	-3 -2 -1 0 1 2 3	-3 -2 -1 0 1 2 3	_____
Hunting	-3 -2 -1 0 1 2 3	-3 -2 -1 0 1 2 3	_____
Ice fishing	-3 -2 -1 0 1 2 3	-3 -2 -1 0 1 2 3	_____
Ice skating	-3 -2 -1 0 1 2 3	-3 -2 -1 0 1 2 3	_____
Jogging	-3 -2 -1 0 1 2 3	-3 -2 -1 0 1 2 3	_____
Judo	-3 -2 -1 0 1 2 3	-3 -2 -1 0 1 2 3	_____
Karate	-3 -2 -1 0 1 2 3	-3 -2 -1 0 1 2 3	_____
Knitting	-3 -2 -1 0 1 2 3	-3 -2 -1 0 1 2 3	_____
Metalwork	-3 -2 -1 0 1 2 3	-3 -2 -1 0 1 2 3	_____
Model building	-3 -2 -1 0 1 2 3	-3 -2 -1 0 1 2 3	_____
Monopoly	-3 -2 -1 0 1 2 3	-3 -2 -1 0 1 2 3	_____
Mountain climbing	-3 -2 -1 0 1 2 3	-3 -2 -1 0 1 2 3	_____
Movies	-3 -2 -1 0 1 2 3	-3 -2 -1 0 1 2 3	_____
Museums	-3 -2 -1 0 1 2 3	-3 -2 -1 0 1 2 3	_____
Opera	-3 -2 -1 0 1 2 3	-3 -2 -1 0 1 2 3	_____
Painting	-3 -2 -1 0 1 2 3	-3 -2 -1 0 1 2 3	_____
Photography	-3 -2 -1 0 1 2 3	-3 -2 -1 0 1 2 3	_____
Pinochle	-3 -2 -1 0 1 2 3	-3 -2 -1 0 1 2 3	_____

Activity	Husband's Rating	Wife's Rating	Total Rating
Plays	-3 -2 -1 0 1 2 3	-3 -2 -1 0 1 2 3	_____
Poetry (writing)	-3 -2 -1 0 1 2 3	-3 -2 -1 0 1 2 3	_____
Polo (watching)	-3 -2 -1 0 1 2 3	-3 -2 -1 0 1 2 3	_____
Pool (or billiards)	-3 -2 -1 0 1 2 3	-3 -2 -1 0 1 2 3	_____
Quilting	-3 -2 -1 0 1 2 3	-3 -2 -1 0 1 2 3	_____
Racquetball	-3 -2 -1 0 1 2 3	-3 -2 -1 0 1 2 3	_____
Remodeling (home)	-3 -2 -1 0 1 2 3	-3 -2 -1 0 1 2 3	_____
Rock collecting	-3 -2 -1 0 1 2 3	-3 -2 -1 0 1 2 3	_____
Roller-skating	-3 -2 -1 0 1 2 3	-3 -2 -1 0 1 2 3	_____
Rowing	-3 -2 -1 0 1 2 3	-3 -2 -1 0 1 2 3	_____
Rummy	-3 -2 -1 0 1 2 3	-3 -2 -1 0 1 2 3	_____
Sailing	-3 -2 -1 0 1 2 3	-3 -2 -1 0 1 2 3	_____
Sculpting	-3 -2 -1 0 1 2 3	-3 -2 -1 0 1 2 3	_____
Shooting (skeet, trap)	-3 -2 -1 0 1 2 3	-3 -2 -1 0 1 2 3	_____
Shooting (pistol)	-3 -2 -1 0 1 2 3	-3 -2 -1 0 1 2 3	_____
Shopping (clothes)	-3 -2 -1 0 1 2 3	-3 -2 -1 0 1 2 3	_____
Shopping (groceries)	-3 -2 -1 0 1 2 3	-3 -2 -1 0 1 2 3	_____
Shopping (vehicles)	-3 -2 -1 0 1 2 3	-3 -2 -1 0 1 2 3	_____
Shopping (_____)	-3 -2 -1 0 1 2 3	-3 -2 -1 0 1 2 3	_____
Shuffleboard	-3 -2 -1 0 1 2 3	-3 -2 -1 0 1 2 3	_____
Sightseeing	-3 -2 -1 0 1 2 3	-3 -2 -1 0 1 2 3	_____
Singing	-3 -2 -1 0 1 2 3	-3 -2 -1 0 1 2 3	_____
Skiing (water)	-3 -2 -1 0 1 2 3	-3 -2 -1 0 1 2 3	_____
Skiing (downhill)	-3 -2 -1 0 1 2 3	-3 -2 -1 0 1 2 3	_____
Skiing (cross-country)	-3 -2 -1 0 1 2 3	-3 -2 -1 0 1 2 3	_____
Skin diving (snorkeling)	-3 -2 -1 0 1 2 3	-3 -2 -1 0 1 2 3	_____
Skydiving	-3 -2 -1 0 1 2 3	-3 -2 -1 0 1 2 3	_____
Snowmobiling	-3 -2 -1 0 1 2 3	-3 -2 -1 0 1 2 3	_____
Softball (watching)	-3 -2 -1 0 1 2 3	-3 -2 -1 0 1 2 3	_____
Softball (playing)	-3 -2 -1 0 1 2 3	-3 -2 -1 0 1 2 3	_____
Spearfishing	-3 -2 -1 0 1 2 3	-3 -2 -1 0 1 2 3	_____
Stamp collecting	-3 -2 -1 0 1 2 3	-3 -2 -1 0 1 2 3	_____
Surfing	-3 -2 -1 0 1 2 3	-3 -2 -1 0 1 2 3	_____
Swimming	-3 -2 -1 0 1 2 3	-3 -2 -1 0 1 2 3	_____
Table tennis	-3 -2 -1 0 1 2 3	-3 -2 -1 0 1 2 3	_____
Taxidermy	-3 -2 -1 0 1 2 3	-3 -2 -1 0 1 2 3	_____

Activity	Husband's Rating	Wife's Rating	Total Rating
Television	−3 −2 −1 0 1 2 3	−3 −2 −1 0 1 2 3	_____
Tennis	−3 −2 −1 0 1 2 3	−3 −2 −1 0 1 2 3	_____
Tobogganing	−3 −2 −1 0 1 2 3	−3 −2 −1 0 1 2 3	_____
Video games	−3 −2 −1 0 1 2 3	−3 −2 −1 0 1 2 3	_____
Video production	−3 −2 −1 0 1 2 3	−3 −2 −1 0 1 2 3	_____
Video movies (watching)	−3 −2 −1 0 1 2 3	−3 −2 −1 0 1 2 3	_____
Volleyball	−3 −2 −1 0 1 2 3	−3 −2 −1 0 1 2 3	_____
Weaving	−3 −2 −1 0 1 2 3	−3 −2 −1 0 1 2 3	_____
Woodworking	−3 −2 −1 0 1 2 3	−3 −2 −1 0 1 2 3	_____
Wrestling (watching)	−3 −2 −1 0 1 2 3	−3 −2 −1 0 1 2 3	_____
Yachting	−3 −2 −1 0 1 2 3	−3 −2 −1 0 1 2 3	_____
_____	−3 −2 −1 0 1 2 3	−3 −2 −1 0 1 2 3	_____
_____	−3 −2 −1 0 1 2 3	−3 −2 −1 0 1 2 3	_____
_____	−3 −2 −1 0 1 2 3	−3 −2 −1 0 1 2 3	_____
_____	−3 −2 −1 0 1 2 3	−3 −2 −1 0 1 2 3	_____
_____	−3 −2 −1 0 1 2 3	−3 −2 −1 0 1 2 3	_____
_____	−3 −2 −1 0 1 2 3	−3 −2 −1 0 1 2 3	_____
_____	−3 −2 −1 0 1 2 3	−3 −2 −1 0 1 2 3	_____
_____	−3 −2 −1 0 1 2 3	−3 −2 −1 0 1 2 3	_____
_____	−3 −2 −1 0 1 2 3	−3 −2 −1 0 1 2 3	_____
_____	−3 −2 −1 0 1 2 3	−3 −2 −1 0 1 2 3	_____
_____	−3 −2 −1 0 1 2 3	−3 −2 −1 0 1 2 3	_____
_____	−3 −2 −1 0 1 2 3	−3 −2 −1 0 1 2 3	_____
_____	−3 −2 −1 0 1 2 3	−3 −2 −1 0 1 2 3	_____
_____	−3 −2 −1 0 1 2 3	−3 −2 −1 0 1 2 3	_____
_____	−3 −2 −1 0 1 2 3	−3 −2 −1 0 1 2 3	_____
_____	−3 −2 −1 0 1 2 3	−3 −2 −1 0 1 2 3	_____
_____	−3 −2 −1 0 1 2 3	−3 −2 −1 0 1 2 3	_____
_____	−3 −2 −1 0 1 2 3	−3 −2 −1 0 1 2 3	_____
_____	−3 −2 −1 0 1 2 3	−3 −2 −1 0 1 2 3	_____
_____	−3 −2 −1 0 1 2 3	−3 −2 −1 0 1 2 3	_____
_____	−3 −2 −1 0 1 2 3	−3 −2 −1 0 1 2 3	_____
_____	−3 −2 −1 0 1 2 3	−3 −2 −1 0 1 2 3	_____
_____	−3 −2 −1 0 1 2 3	−3 −2 −1 0 1 2 3	_____

Appendix D

Financial Support Inventory

Needs and Wants Budget

This budget is designed to help clarify the need for financial support. The spouse with this need is to complete this questionnaire.

Please create three budgets in the spaces provided under the three columns. Under the Needs Budget column, indicate the monthly cost of meeting the necessities of your life, items you would be uncomfortable without. In the Income section, only your spouse's income should appear in the column.

Under the Wants Budget column, indicate the cost of meeting your needs and your wants—reasonable desires that would be more costly than necessities. These desires should be as realistic as possible. They should not include a new house, a new car, or luxuries, unless you have been wanting these items for some time. Both your income and your spouse's income should appear in this column.

The Affordable Budget column should include all the Needs amounts and only the Wants amounts that can be covered by you and your spouse's income. In other words, your income should equal your expenses, and the Income Minus Expenses item at the end of the Affordable Budget column should be zero. This Affordable Budget should be used to guide your household finances if both you and your spouse have agreed to the amounts listed.

Payments from the past few months (or year if possible) will help you arrive at correct estimates. Use monthly averages for items that are not paid monthly, such as repairs, vacations, and gifts. Some items, such as your mortgage payment, will be the same amount for both your Needs and Wants budgets. Other items, such as vacation expense, will be much more a Want than a Need. It is highly recommended that you include in your Needs Budget an emergency expense item that is 10 percent of your total budget. In months with no emergency expenses, it should be saved for the future. Most households suffer needless financial stress when they fail to budget for inevitable emergencies. If you can think of other significant expenses, include these in the blank spaces provided.

If your spouse's income is equal to or greater than the total expenses in the Needs Budget column, it's sufficient to pay for your Needs, and it's meeting your need for financial support. It may actually be covering some of your Wants as well. This may not have been obvious, since you have not been dividing your bills into Needs and Wants. Your need for financial support is still being met when your income is used to pay for Wants that are not covered by your spouse's income.

However, if your spouse's income is insufficient to pay for your Needs, either you must reduce your household expenses without sacrificing your basic needs, or he must increase his income with a pay raise, a new job, or a new career to meet these needs.

You have the permission of the publisher to photocopy the questionnaire for use in your own marriage. I recommend that you enlarge it 125 percent so that you'll have plenty of room to write in your responses.

Household Expenses and Income	Needs Budget	Wants Budget	Affordable Budget
Expenses			
Taxes			
Income tax	_____	_____	_____
Property tax	_____	_____	_____
Other taxes	_____	_____	_____
Interest			
Mortgage interest	_____	_____	_____
Credit card interest	_____	_____	_____
Automobile loan interest	_____	_____	_____
Other interest	_____	_____	_____
Insurance			
Homeowner's insurance	_____	_____	_____
Life insurance	_____	_____	_____

Household Expenses and Income	Needs Budget	Wants Budget	Affordable Budget
Liability insurance			
Auto insurance			
Medical and dental insurance			
Other insurance			
Home Expenses			
Home repair			
Home remodeling			
Home security			
Home cleaning			
Yard maintenance			
Fuel (gas and electricity)			
Telephone			
Garbage removal			
Other Home Expenses			
Furniture and Appliances			
Furniture purchase			
Appliance purchase			
Furniture and appliance repair			
Automobiles			
Husband's auto depreciation			
Husband's auto fuel			
Husband's auto maintenance			
Wife's auto depreciation			
Wife's auto fuel			
Wife's auto maintenance			
Other auto expenses			
Food and Entertainment			
Groceries			
Dining out			

Household Expenses and Income	Needs Budget	Wants Budget	Affordable Budget
Vacation			
Recreational boat expense			
Photography			
Magazines and newspapers			
Cable TV			
Other food and entertainment			
Health			
Medical (over insurance)			
Dental (over insurance)			
Nonprescription drugs			
Exercise expense			
Special diet expense			
Other health expenses			
Clothing			
Husband's clothing purchases			
Wife's clothing purchases			
Children's clothing purchases			
Dry cleaning			
Alterations and repairs			
Other clothing expenses			
Personal			
Husband's allowance			
Wife's allowance			
Children's allowances			
Gifts			
Religious contributions (tithe, religious organizations)			

Household Expenses and Income	Needs Budget	Wants Budget	Affordable Budget
Nonreligious contributions (other charitable causes)	_____	_____	_____
Gifts for special events (birthdays, Christmas, etc.)	_____	_____	_____
Pets			
Pet food	_____	_____	_____
Veterinary expense	_____	_____	_____
Other pet expense	_____	_____	_____
Savings			
Savings for children's education	_____	_____	_____
Savings for retirement (IRAs)	_____	_____	_____
Savings for other projects	_____	_____	_____
Other Household Expenses			
Banking	_____	_____	_____
Legal	_____	_____	_____
Accounting and tax preparation	_____	_____	_____
Emergency fund (10%)	_____	_____	_____
_____	_____	_____	_____
Total Household Expenses	_____	_____	_____
Income			
Husband's salary	_____	_____	_____
Husband's other income	_____	_____	_____
Wife's salary	_____	_____	_____
Wife's other income	_____	_____	_____
Investment income	_____	_____	_____
Interest income	_____	_____	_____
_____	_____	_____	_____
Total Household Income	_____	_____	_____
Income Minus Expenses	_____	_____	_____

Dr. Willard F. Harley, Jr., is a nationally acclaimed clinical psychologist, marriage counselor, and bestselling author. His popular website, www.marriagebuilders.com, offers practical solutions to almost any marital problem. Dr. Harley and his wife, Joyce, host a daily radio call-in show, *Marriage Builders*. They live in White Bear Lake, Minnesota.

The best book on marriage is now *better than ever!*

For over twenty-five years, *His Needs, Her Needs* has been transforming marriages all over the world. Now this life-changing book is the basis for an interactive six-week DVD study designed for use in couples' small groups or retreats, in premarital counseling sessions, or by individual couples.

Revell
a division of Baker Publishing Group
www.RevellBooks.com

Available Wherever Books Are Sold
Also Available in Ebook Format

Take the next step to strengthen your marriage.

Through the process of "joint agreement" you and your spouse can make decisions together and both get what you want and believe is best—every time.

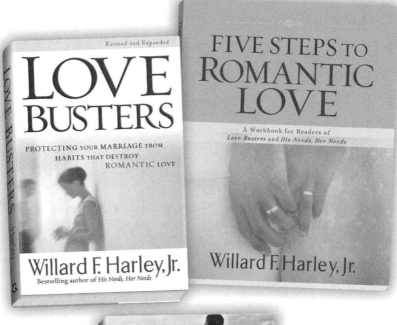

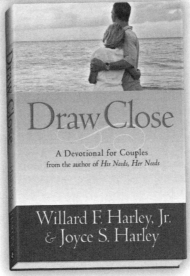

The strength of your marriage depends on the
passion you share with each other. These three books will
draw you closer together.

ENJOY A ROMANTIC, PASSIONATE, *lifelong marriage!*

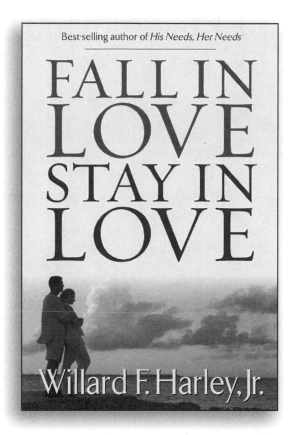

D
r. Harley has spent more than thirty years helping couples create, re-create, and sustain romantic love. In this foundational book, he provides you with all the tools you'll need to fall in love and stay in love with your spouse.